You will love all the soical studies projects we do!

- Greyson Verhoff

D1060163

Cardinal

Buckeye

Flint   Red Carnation   Ladybug   Trilobite

Ohio's State Symbols

Contents

Maps and Diagrams

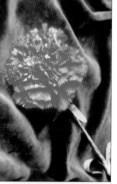

Chapter 1

Chapter 1

Ohio's Land

WORDS TO UNDERSTAND

geography
continent
country
natural environment
habitat
human features
climate
average
temperate
humid
precipitation
geologist
sediment
erode
glacier
divide
extinct
region
till
preserve

What kind of a place is Ohio? Where do the people live? How do they use and change the land?

Photo by Scott Barrow

The Land We Call Home

Ohio seems very large. Yet it is just one small part of the world. Because we live in Ohio, it is important to us. It is our home. Millions of people all over the world live in places that are important to them.

In this chapter you will begin to learn about Ohio by studying its *geography*. Geography is the study of the land, water, plants, animals, and people of a place. Geography tells us where places are, and what they are like. It teaches us about the relationships between the people and the land.

Why is it important to know about the geography of a place? Because geography affects where we live and how we live. People usually live on flat land where they can build homes and larger buildings for businesses. Cities nearly always started

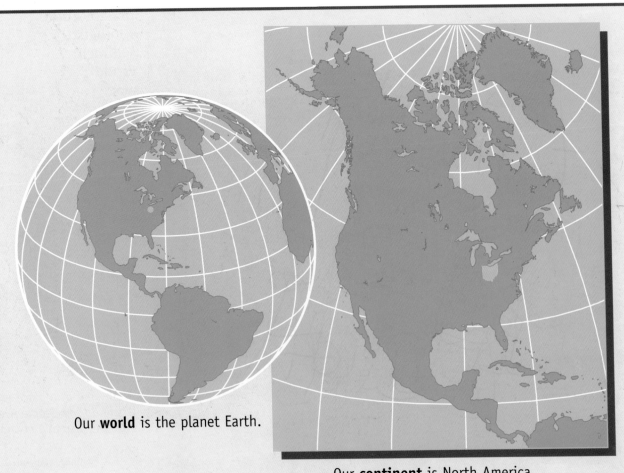

Our **world** is the planet Earth.

Our **continent** is North America.

near a river or a lake. The people needed the water for drinking, cooking, washing, and industry. It is also easier to farm on flat or gently rolling hills than on steeper cliffs or in rocky places.

Where in the World Are We?

We all know we live on planet Earth. But just where on planet Earth do we live? Ohio is located on one of the world's *continents*. Continents are very large land areas. Most of them have oceans on many sides. Ohio is on the continent of North America.

Ohio is part of a *country* on that continent. A country is a land region under the control of one government. Our country is the United States of America. Canada is the country to the north of us. Mexico is the country to the south of us.

Our **country** is the United States of America.

Our **state** is Ohio.

Lines around the World

Every place in the world has an exact location that is measured by *latitude* and *longitude* lines. You can find these lines on a map or a globe.

Latitude lines run east and west (side to side on the map).

Longitude lines run north and south (up and down on the map).

Along the lines you will find numbers. Each number has a tiny circle by it. This is a *symbol* for a *degree*. A degree is a part of a circle or globe.

The degree numbers all begin at 0. The *equator* is 0 degrees latitude. Find the line that is 0 degrees longitude. It is called the *prime meridian*. Find these lines on the globe. The degree numbers get larger as they move farther away from the equator and the prime meridian.

North Pole

Prime Meridian

Ohio

Equator

Activity

Where Is Ohio?

On this map, find Ohio's **latitude** and **longitude** lines. Use a globe in your classroom to trace these lines all the way around the world.

1. Which longitude line is near the western border of the state?
2. Locate about where you live on the map. What is your longitude and latitude?

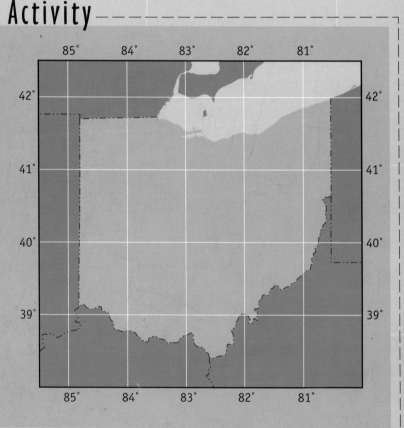

6

Place: What Kind of Place is Ohio?

All places are like other places in some ways. All places are different in some ways. All places have a *natural environment*. The natural environment includes such things as lakes, rivers, plains, hills, and even plants and animals.

Ohio is a place of flat plains and rugged hills. Many kinds of plants and animals live on both kinds of land. They are part of our natural environment.

Places also have *human features*. People change the environment by clearing forests to make room for roads and towns. People build strong bridges over rivers. They build dams across the rivers to stop flooding. They plant apple and peach orchards throughout Ohio. Human features include big cities like Cleveland, Cincinnati, Columbus, Dayton, and Toledo.

The natural home of a plant or animal is called a *habitat*.

The Falls in Sharon Woods Gorge are just one of many natural features found in Ohio.
Photo by Tom Till

People change the land by building cities. This is Toledo.

Land of Many Waters

Lake Erie

Maumee R.

Blanchard R.

Sandusky R.

Cuyahoga R.

Great Miami R.

Little Miami R.

Muskingum R.

Hocking R.

Scioto R.

Ohio River

Ohio River

Ohio sits between two great bodies of water. There is the Ohio River to the south, and Lake Erie to the north. The Ohio River begins high in the mountains of Pennsylvania. Here the Allegheny and Monongahela Rivers come together to form the Ohio River. It then flows a thousand miles to the Mississippi River. In most places, it runs two miles wide through steep cliffs and wooded hillsides.

The Beautiful River

The Ohio River gave its name to the state. The Indians called the river Oyo (Oh-HEE-oh). This meant deep or great river. When the French explorer LaSalle first saw the river, he understood the Indian word "Oyo" to mean the French word "belle" or beautiful. He called the Ohio River "La Belle Riviere (la-BELL-rih-vee-EHR)" or the Beautiful River. From then on, the word "Ohio" meant both the beautiful river and the beautiful country running north of it to Lake Erie.

Canada geese take a break in the Maumee River during the winter season.
Photo by Art Weber

Fishing for bass on the Ohio River is a popular sport.
Photo by Art Weber

Lake Erie

Lake Erie was named for the Erie Indians who used to live along its shore. It is one of the five Great Lakes.

The water of all the Great Lakes is fresh water—it has no salt. The shoreline of Lake Erie is mainly rocky with a few sandy beaches, marshy wetlands, and fine harbors.

The lake is important as a water supply for both people and industry. The lake is also important for fishing, recreation, and tourism.

In between the Ohio River and Lake Erie, the state has more than 40,000 miles of rivers and streams. Ohio also has a few natural lakes and many man-made lakes.

Marblehead Lighthouse shines at sunset on Lake Erie.
Photo by Tom Till

9

That's a Fact!

Did you know that many rivers in Ohio are named after the American Indian tribes who lived near them? The Great Miami, Little Miami, and Maumee are all named for the Miami Indians. The Tuscawaras River is named for the Tuscaroras—a tribe of the Iroquois Nation.

The Indians also gave names to the rivers. See what the names of these rivers mean in the Indian languages.

- Sandusky River – Water within water pools
- Cuyahoga River – Place of the wing
- Muskingum River – Glint in the eye of the elk
- Scioto River – River of the deer hair
- Olentangy River – River with flat stones along its shore
- Hocking River – Bottleneck of tree logs
- Auglaize River – Falling timbers

Winter snow is beautiful to look at.

What season is it in this picture?

Photo by Tom Till

Our Climate

Climate is very important to a place. *Climate* is what the weather of a place is like over a long period of time. The *average* amount of rain or snow that falls in your yard is part of the climate. The average temperatures in summer and winter when you want to play outside are part of climate.

Ohio is known for its varied climate. The summers can be very hot and humid. Heavy rains come in spring and autumn. Tornadoes often hit the state in the spring and early summer. Floods can occur along Ohio's many rivers. In the winter, the wind blows cold and blizzards bring many inches of snow.

Compared with the weather in the rest of the world, Ohio's climate is considered *temperate*. This means it is neither too hot nor too cold. Many Ohioans might be surprised to learn this!

In the summer, you probably hear people complaining that the air is too *humid*. This means there are tiny drops of moisture in the air. Other moisture that falls to the ground in the form of rain and snow is called *precipitation*.

More snow than the average falls in an area called the Snow Belt. It includes the land along Lake Erie from Cleveland to Pennsylvania. Here the clouds and cold wind off the lake can bring over 100 inches of snow each year!

Ohio in the Making

Geologists are scientists who study the formation of the earth. They believe that it took millions of years to shape Ohio's landforms and climate. Geologists believe that hundreds of millions of years ago, much of North America was covered by an ocean. Many creatures like trilobites, sharks, and oysters lived in this great salty sea.

The ocean built up *sediment* (deposits of sand and minerals) over the rock beneath the water. These layers of sediment *eroded*, or washed away, and then built up again. In the process, important minerals were laid down one on top of the other. Dolomite, gypsum, sand, and rock salt formed first. Later limestone, flint, clay, and sandstone were deposited.

The great ocean finally went away. The land was more like a tropical forest than the Ohio we know today. Ferns grew over seventy feet high. Locusts buzzed in the trees. Dragonflies with wingspans of more than two feet glided through the forest.

After the ancient plants and animals died, they were covered with layers of dirt and the remains of more living things. Pressure from all that weight, as well as the heat under the ground, changed the living matter into coal and oil.

Fossils are prints or remains of plants or animals in rock. When geologists study fossils, they learn about life long ago.

The Amazing Locust

Have you ever heard locusts buzzing in the trees? Usually around the Fourth of July, the locusts begin their summer call. Have you heard people say, "The locusts are singing. That means six more weeks until cold weather!"

This is an old folk tale. The amazing insect has been in Ohio for millions of years!

The trilobite is one of the earliest fossils. Trilobites and snails lived here millions of years ago.

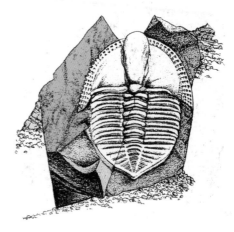

Limestone is used in concrete and fertilizer. This limestone deposit is near Manchester.

Flint Ridge

Flint Ridge had one of the greatest flint deposits in the world.

Natural Resources

How do we use our natural resources today?

- Dolomite – Bricks and fertilizer
- Gypsum – Plasterboard
- Sand – Glass
- Rock Salt – Water softener and winter road salt
- Limestone – Concrete and fertilizer
- Flint – Grindstones
- Clay – Pipes and pottery
- Sandstone – Building
- Coal – Fuel and energy
- Oil – Fuel and energy

Our State Gem

Flint is our state gem. It is a kind of quartz. One of the greatest flint deposits in the world was at a place called Flint Ridge. That's in Licking County near Columbus.

Ohio Indians were the first to discover shiny veins of flint along the ridge. They mined the flint and made arrowheads and spearheads from it. They traded the flint with tribes as far east as the Atlantic Ocean and as far west as the Mississippi River. Later settlers used the flint to make heavy millstones that ground their wheat into flour.

You can still go to Flint Ridge today. It is now a state park with hiking trails and places to picnic.

Flint is our state gem, or stone. How did the early American Indians use flint? How did the pioneers use flint?

Glaciers Shaped the Land

Our rich soil is a valuable natural resource. The soil was brought here during the Ice Age. About 25,000 years ago, the earth became very cold. Glaciers came south from Canada and covered much of North America. A *glacier* is a huge moving mountain of ice. In some places, the ice was more than a mile thick!

The glaciers came, melted, then came again for about 6,000 years. Then they melted and moved northward, changing the land. The moving ice ground down jagged mountains into smooth rolling hills and flat plains. As they melted, the glaciers deposited the rich soil they had carried from Canada.

The glaciers also left a ridge of low hills called a *divide*. To this day, rivers north of the divide flow into Lake Erie. Those rivers south of the divide flow into the Ohio River.

Glaciers covered much of Ohio. The Great Lakes were formed from the water of melting glaciers.

Rivers flowing north of the divide are shown in purple.
Rivers flowing south of the divide are shown in red.

Kelleys Island: Retreating glaciers left grooves in the limestone on Kelleys Island. The grooves are a few inches to many feet deep!

Photo by Art Weber

Mammoths were some of the largest Ice Age animals.

Ice Age Animals

In the last days of the Ice Age, huge mammoths lived in the tall cedar forests. Mammoths were much larger than today's elephants. They could be fourteen feet tall. They had long shaggy fur that hung almost to the ground. Strands of fur were three feet long. Fossils with curved tusks more than thirteen feet long have been found here.

There were other Ice Age animals, too. Giant camels, small horses, and huge bison ate the green grasses and leaves of bushes and trees. Large cats were meat-eating animals.

As the weather got warmer and warmer, and as early people came to live on the land, all of these animals became *extinct*. They never lived on the earth again.

Plain:
wide level area of land

Wetland:
area that is usually soaked with water

Peninsula:
land that has water on three sides

Bay:
body of water that curves into a coastline

Land Regions

A region is another way to tell about a place. Geographers divide large areas of the world into smaller parts. We call these parts *regions*. Regions are places that have certain things in common, or that are alike in some way. Ohio has four main regions: the Lake Plain, the Till Plains, the Bluegrass Region, and the Appalachian Plateau. Each region has mostly one type of landform, though it can have others. The main landforms in Ohio's four regions are plains and hills.

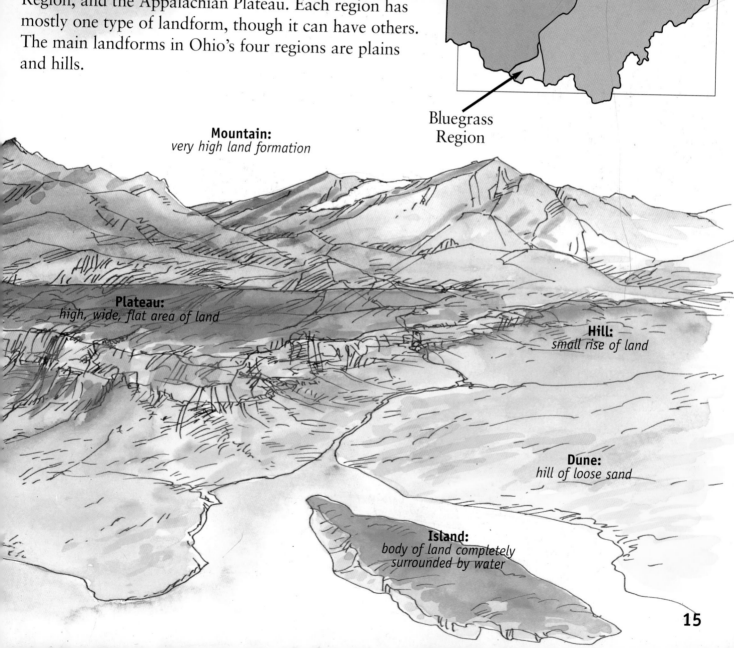

Ohio's Land Regions

Lake Plain

Till Plains

Appalachian Plateau

Bluegrass Region

Mountain:
very high land formation

Plateau:
high, wide, flat area of land

Hill:
small rise of land

Dune:
hill of loose sand

Island:
body of land completely surrounded by water

15

The Lake Plain Region

This region stretches along the southern edge of Lake Erie. A long time ago, this region was part of an ancient lake. That is why so much of the soil is made of clay. The lake deposited the clay as it moved northward. You can still see sandy ridges called oak openings. They are the remains of the old lake shore. Oak trees love to grow in the ancient sand.

The soil of the entire Lake Plain region is good for farming. Corn, wheat, apples, tomatoes, peaches, and even grapes grow throughout the Lake Plain. The lake shore also provides harbors where big cities such as Cleveland and Toledo trade with the world.

Lake Erie is a good place for people to vacation in the summer. Sandusky is an important tourist center. It is home to the Cedar Point Amusement Park. People come from all over the world to ride the park's many roller coasters.

Even though many people live in the Lake Plain, it is still home to many animals and plants. Migrating birds come in the spring and fall to marshy places along the lake called wetlands.

Cleveland is one of the largest cities in the Lake Plain Region.
Photo by F. Moegling

The Maumee River provides harbors for world trade in Toledo.

The sand dunes at Oak Openings Preserve are a great place to visit.
Photo by Art Weber

You can go to the many state parks along the Lake Erie shore to watch the birds gather. Look up and you might see eagles, hawks, and falcons circling in the warm air. Look down and you might see blue herons, turtles, and leopard frogs in the marshes. Walk along the beaches and see if you can spot birds called killdeers hiding in the purple sandgrass.

The Black Swamp

Photo by Roberta Stockwell

Did you ever ride the Magnum Rollercoaster at Cedar Point?

Peaches are grown in the Lake Plain Region.

The Lake Erie Islands

Ohio has twelve islands in Lake Erie. A few thousand people live on Kelleys Island and South and Middle Bass Islands all year. There are many grape vineyards and peach orchards there, too. Kelleys Island is also an important source of limestone.

The population of the Lake Erie Islands swells in the summertime. Boaters, fishermen, and tourists come to vacation along the lake. Wildlife is also important. Brown bats, ring-billed gulls, and mudpuppy salamanders all find a home on the Lake Erie Islands.

A great blue heron chick looks for food.
Photo by Jim Oltersdorf

For many years, the northwest corner of this region was called the Black Swamp. All along the Maumee River, a tangle of tall trees blocked out the sun. The forest floor was covered with water year round. Mosquitoes made life miserable for people and animals alike. Farmers finally drained the Black Swamp and found rich soil for planting.

The Till Plains Region

The Till Plains is another important region in the state. A long time ago, glaciers left rich *till*, or soil, behind as they melted. The soil of this region is rich and fertile. The land is very flat with only a few rolling hills.

This region is on the edge of a great farming region called the Corn Belt. The Corn Belt stretches west to Illinois and Iowa. Large farms growing corn and wheat in the deep black soil can be seen for miles and miles throughout much of the Till Plains.

Oats, barley, red clover, rye, and timothy grass also grow tall in the warm summers. Most of these crops are fed to the many cows, pigs, and horses that are raised in the Till Plains. Farmers grow cabbages, onions, potatoes, tomatoes, and apples.

Popcorn is one of the best-selling crops in this region. Remember the next time you are watching a movie and eating popcorn that the corn might have been grown on a farm in Ohio's rich Till Plains!

Harvesting corn is big business in Ohio's Till Plains.

This wheatfield is found in the Till Plains region.

Photo by Terry Cartwright

Farmers raise cows in the Till Plains.

Photo by John Ivanko

Columbus is Ohio's state capital.
Photo by John Ivanko

Although farming is very important to the region, many large cities dot the rolling plains. Columbus, the state capital, is near the Olentangy River. Dayton is on the Miami River. Cincinnati sits on the Ohio River.

Compared with the other regions of the state, there are fewer wild animals in the Till Plains. Farmers have cleared so much land for planting that only animals who can adapt to the open spaces live here. Many cottontail rabbits, meadowlarks, garter snakes, green tree frogs, and swallowtail butterflies make their home in the fields.

Cincinnati is a busy city at all hours of the night.
Photo by David J. Castielli

Dayton is reflected in the Miami River.
Photo by Terry Cartwright

19

The Appalachian Plateau Region

The largest region of the state is called the Appalachian or, Allegheny Plateau. It includes nearly one-half of the state. It is formed by the western edge of the Allegheny Mountains.

Long ago, glaciers covered only the edge of the Appalachian Plateau. As the glaciers melted and moved northward, they left good soil behind. They rounded off the high mountaintops. Today there are many farms and much good pasture land in this part of the plateau. More people and industries can be found here than in any other part of the state.

Forests of cedar and beech trees grow here. In the spring, syrup is made from the sap of sugar maple trees. In the fall, the leaves of the many trees turn bright shades of orange, red, and yellow.

This region is an important habitat for wildlife. White-tailed deer, box turtles, and monarch butterflies find a home in the forests and pasture land.

Where the Glaciers Never Came

Glaciers never came into the part of the Appalachian Plateau called the hill country. It is a region of steep gorges, deep streams, and many rocky ledges with tumbling waterfalls.

Farmers were first disappointed when they came into this region. The soil was poor and it was hard to grow crops. Later Ohioans discovered rich deposits of coal, iron, and clay. These are valuable materials for modern industry. People cut down nearly all the trees. They tore the hillsides apart digging for the rich mineral deposits.

The hill country is finally returning to its natural state. The hills and valleys are again covered with thick forests of oak, hickory, maple, elm, and sycamore trees. Black bears, gray squirrels, and copperhead snakes are returning to their old home. The Hocking Hills along the Ohio River is considered by many people to be the most beautiful part of the state. In the fall, people come from all over to see the bright colors of the leaves and to watch the birds migrating southward.

The white-tailed deer is Ohio's state animal.
Photo by Jim Oltersdorf

This scene near Cambridge shows the peaceful landscape of the region. Glaciers smoothed out the land into gently rolling hills.
Photo by Art Weber

Old Man's Cave State Park is in the Hocking Hills. The glaciers never came here, so the land is rugged.
Photo by Tom Till

Coal is a valuable resource. This is Wayne Mine near Holmesville.

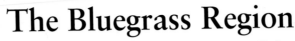

The Bluegrass Region

Along the Ohio River, you will find another important region of Ohio. It is called the Lexington Plain or the Bluegrass Region. It is the smallest region in the state. This region looks just like the state of Kentucky across the Ohio River. Fields of tall bluegrass grow. There are many flat-topped hills and cliffs along the creeks.

The region's prairies and cedar forests are home to some of the rarest species of plants and animals in Ohio. Wild turkeys, wood rats, salamanders, lizards, and blue butterflies can be spotted in the region. It is also a good place to watch songbirds migrating north in the spring and hawks flying south in the fall.

While there are no major cities in this area, there are many farms. Tobacco is the main crop. It grows well in the rich soil during the long warm growing season.

Have you ever seen a blue butterfly?
Photo by Art Weber

An old barn is located in the Bluegrass Region.
Photo by Kathleen Stockwell

Our Changing Land

Geographers study the relationship between the land and people, plants, and animals over time. Our land is always changing. Some change is very slow. Erosion and wind slowly wear away rock and soil. Some change is very fast. Natural events such as floods and tornadoes can change the land quickly.

People also change the land. They cut down the trees. They build cities and roads. They plant crops. They use fertilizers to make crops grow. They dig into the ground for natural resources such as coal and oil. They use herbicides to kill weeds and pesticides to kill insects. They cut away sandstone to use for building. These things can be important for people. They provide things we all need, like homes and jobs. We have to be careful, though, to keep the land, water, and air clean and beautiful.

No one wants to live where there is trash on the ground. Never litter. Pick up garbage that spills. It is up to all of us to keep our land clean.

In 1974 a tornado tore through Xenia. The tornado lasted for only a few minutes. The damage was terrible. Thirty people were killed. The forces of nature often change the land.

23

A Young Man Remembers Wild Ohio

A young man named David Zeisberger came to Ohio when it was still a wilderness. He was a Christian missionary. He came to teach the Ohio Indians about his religion.

When he was older, he wrote a book about what Ohio looked like when he first saw it. He remembered buffalo, elk, and white-tailed deer grazing in large herds. Black bears would "climb trees and bring down chestnuts and acorns" to eat. Panthers, wolves, and foxes lurked in the forests. Passenger pigeons flew overhead in huge flocks that darkened the sky. Beavers built dams in the creeks so large that "they might have been built by human hands."

Forests covered almost all of Ohio. Beech, maple, buckeye, hickory, and birch trees grew tall. Trunks of oak trees rose fifty feet before branching. A man could walk more than sixty paces around the bottom of one of these oak trees. Sycamores grew so tall that people and their horses could take shelter from storms in their hollowed-out trunks.

But Zeisberger saw Ohio changing even then. People hunted the beaver and deer until there were few left. Later they cut down nearly all the trees to build farms. The buffalo and elk left Ohio. Many animals like the black bears, foxes, panthers, beavers, and passenger pigeons were killed. Some wild animals like the gray squirrel and the cardinal were captured and kept by children as pets. The hill country was dug up as people searched for minerals.

Within a hundred years of David Zeisberger's first look at Ohio, the wilderness had disappeared!

David Zeisberger
1721–1808

People change the land by clearing trees to make roads. This is an early pioneer trail.
Photo by Kathleen Stockwell

24

Wild Ohio Returns

Ohio is changing again. Did you know that Ohio today looks more like the wild Ohio of the past than it did a hundred years ago? The people of Ohio have worked hard to restore their state to its natural beauty. Forests have been replanted. Some herbicides and pesticides are no longer used. Parks, wetlands, and nature *preserves* have been set aside to protect wild plants and animals. Many native animals such as the black bear, wild turkey, and red fox are living in Ohio again.

Sadly, some animals such as the panther and passenger pigeon will never return. They are extinct.

This red fox lives in Ohio.

Passenger pigeons are extinct. They will never live here again.

Ohio's wild bats are insectivores. They only eat things like moths, beetles, and mosquitoes. Bats won't and don't attack, so you don't have to worry about one getting tangled up in your hair!

Photo by Jim Oltersdorf

Ohio Portrait

Photo by Jim Oltersdorf

Bald Eagles Are Back!

Long ago travelers to the Ohio wilderness spotted many bald eagles. "The eagle has a white head and tail," wrote young David Zeisberger. He saw how the eagles loved high places. The eagle "builds its nest usually in the fork of some lofty tree . . . and repairs the nest built there every spring."

The bald eagles disappeared from Ohio when their habitat was destroyed. Just twenty years ago, there were only four nesting pairs left in the state.

But now the bald eagle is back! The Ohio Division of Wildlife has raised baby eaglets and placed them in wild nests. This is called "fostering." The adult eagles have taken care of the baby eagles.

The population is now thriving. Baby eagles are being born in the wild. Eagles have been spotted all along the Lake Erie shore. They have even been seen along the Maumee River.

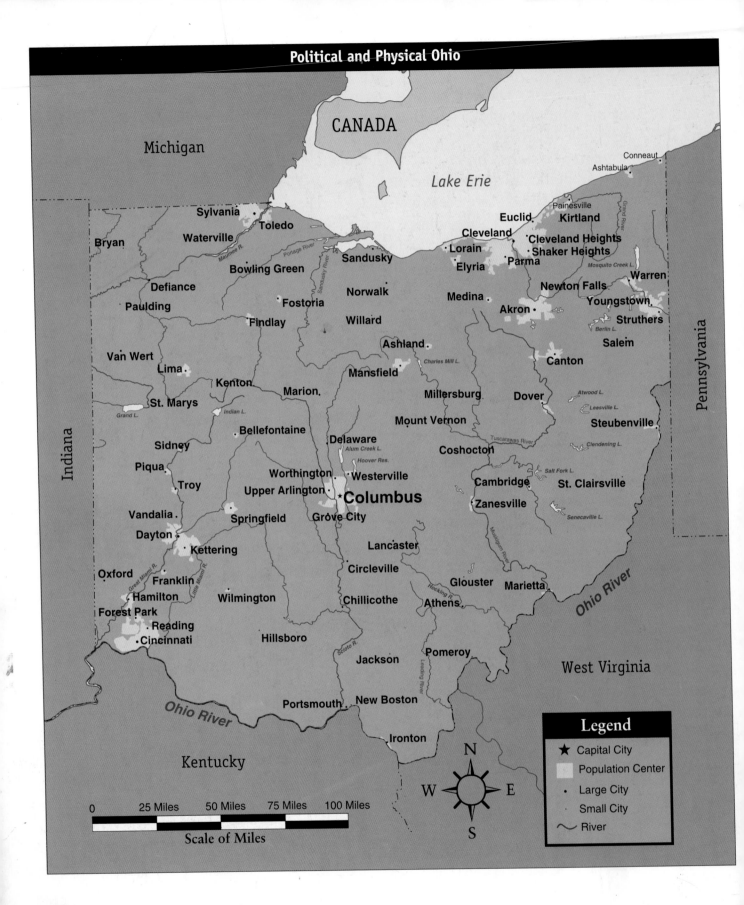

Political and Physical Ohio

Michigan

CANADA

Lake Erie

Conneaut
Ashtabula

Sylvania
Toledo
Waterville

Bryan

Euclid
Painesville
Kirtland
Cleveland
Cleveland Heights
Lorain
Shaker Heights
Elyria
Parma

Warren

Sandusky

Bowling Green

Defiance

Norwalk

Medina

Newton Falls
Youngstown

Fostoria

Paulding

Findlay

Willard

Akron

Struthers

Salem

Van Wert

Ashland

Charles Mill L.

Canton

Lima

Mansfield

Kenton

Marion

Millersburg

Dover

Atwood L.

Leesville L.

St. Marys

Grand L.

Indian L.

Mount Vernon

Coshocton

Tuscarawas River

Clendening L.

Steubenville

Sidney

Bellefontaine

Delaware
Alum Creek L.
Hoover Res.

Piqua

Troy

Worthington

Westerville

Cambridge

St. Clairsville

Salt Fork L.

Upper Arlington

★ **Columbus**

Zanesville

Vandalia

Springfield

Grove City

Senecaville L.

Dayton

Kettering

Lancaster

Oxford

Franklin

Circleville

Glouster

Marietta

Hamilton

Wilmington

Chillicothe

Athens

Hocking R.

Ohio River

Forest Park

Reading

Cincinnati

Hillsboro

Scioto R.

Jackson

Pomeroy

Leading River

West Virginia

Portsmouth

New Boston

Ironton

Kentucky

Indiana

Pennsylvania

Grand River

Mosquito Creek L.

Berlin L.

Maumee R.

Portage River

Sandusky River

Great Miami R.

Little Miami R.

Muskingum River

Legend

★ Capital City

Population Center

• Large City

Small City

~ River

N
W E
S

0   25 Miles   50 Miles   75 Miles   100 Miles

Scale of Miles

26

Reading a Map

There are many kinds of maps. Can you think of some? Perhaps you first thought of a road map. You might use it on a vacation trip. Maps help us get to where we want to go. They show us where places are. Most maps have **symbols** you need to know. Here are some of them:

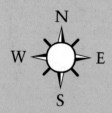

Compass: The directions north, south, east, and west are called cardinal directions. Directions between these, such as northeast or southwest, are called intermediate directions. Most maps have north at the top. It helps to read a map if you put the map so that you are facing north. Then west will be on your left, and east will be on your right. Where will south be? Southwest? Northwest?

Legend or Key: Mapmakers use symbols to stand for certain things such as rivers or cities. Whenever there are symbols, there is a **key** or **legend** that explains what the symbols mean. What do the symbols on this legend represent?

Scale of Miles: To show us distances, or how far apart places really are, mapmakers use a **scale of miles**. One inch on a map might mean 100 miles, 1,000 miles, or even more. About how many miles is it from Toledo to Columbus? Which is the shorter distance: from Columbus to Cincinnati or from Cleveland to Akron?

Chapter 1 Review

1. What continent do we live on?
2. What country do we live in?
3. What state do we live in?
4. Name three things in our natural environment.
5. Why is our state called "Ohio"?
6. Climate is the _____ over a long period of time.
7. Coal and oil are made from ancient _____ and _____.
8. Glaciers smoothed out our land and deposited rich _____.
9. Ohio is divided into _____ land regions.
10. Name two natural ways our land changes.

Geography Tie-In

Landforms such as rivers, lakes, mountains, and hills form **natural boundaries** between states. People decide where **political boundaries** should be. You can't see them in nature. They are lines drawn on a map.
1. What two bodies of water form Ohio's natural boundaries?
2. What five states form a political boundary with Ohio? (Use the map on page 6.)
3. What other country forms a political boundary with Ohio?

The First People

Timeline of Events

13,000 B.C.–7,000 B.C.
Paleo-Indians

13,000 B.C.   11,500 B.C.   10,000 B.C.   8,500 B.C.   1,000

8,000 B.C.–500 B.C.
Archaic Indians

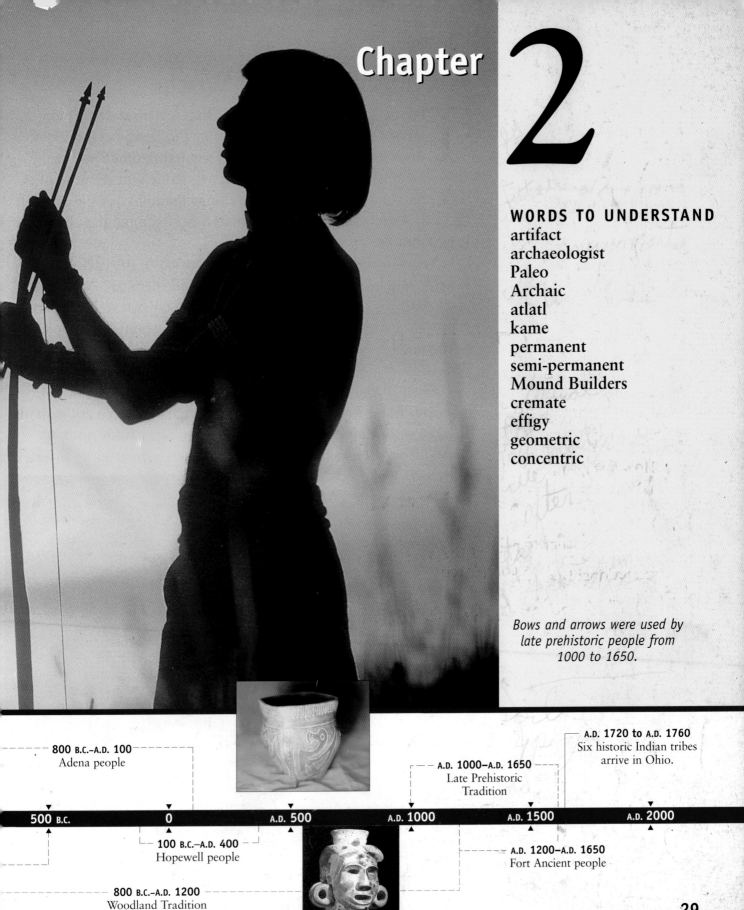

Chapter 2

WORDS TO UNDERSTAND
artifact
archaeologist
Paleo
Archaic
atlatl
kame
permanent
semi-permanent
Mound Builders
cremate
effigy
geometric
concentric

*Bows and arrows were used by
late prehistoric people from
1000 to 1650.*

800 B.C.–A.D. 100
Adena people

A.D. 1000–A.D. 1650
Late Prehistoric
Tradition

A.D. 1720 to A.D. 1760
Six historic Indian tribes
arrive in Ohio.

500 B.C.   0   A.D. 500   A.D. 1000   A.D. 1500   A.D. 2000

100 B.C.–A.D. 400
Hopewell people

A.D. 1200–A.D. 1650
Fort Ancient people

800 B.C.–A.D. 1200
Woodland Tradition

Archaeologists at Work

The people who first lived in Ohio left no written records about their lives. However, they did leave behind clues that tell us how they lived. They left *artifacts* in burial sites and trash piles. They left rock art, stone and ceramic pots, tools, and clothing. Artifacts are things made by people and left behind. *Archaeologists* are scientists who examine the clues to learn how the people lived.

Most of the ancient artifacts are buried in the earth. Over time, layers of sand and dirt have covered them up. Archaeologists must dig slowly and carefully. They try not to break tiny bones or artifacts that will help them learn about the people. Sometimes only a small brush is gentle enough to remove the dirt.

Most of the work of an archaeologist is slow and not very exciting. But every now and then, an amazing discovery is made. Instead of finding only ashes, an archaeologist finds human bones. Could this skeleton once have been a great king, priest, or warrior?

The entire person glittered with shell and copper . . . a thousand beads, many of them pearl, were strewn about everywhere . . . upon the head was a helmet of copper with wooden antlers covered by more copper . . . all hammered out by hand!

Archaeologists dig very slowly and carefully, trying not to break tiny bones or artifacts that will help them learn about ancient people.

Paleo-Indian People

The first people to come to North America hunted huge wild animals for food. Mammoths, caribou, oxen, and wolves are animals that do well in cold climates. Some people followed these animals south to Mexico and beyond. Others traveled eastward. They crossed the Mississippi River and journeyed all along the Ohio River Valley.

Today we call these people Paleo-Indians, though that is not what they called themselves. *Paleo* means ancient. The Paleo-Indians hunted large and small animals with spears. They gathered seeds, nuts, and roots from many wild plants.

Women and men used bone needles to sew animal hides together. The hides were used for clothes and blankets.

When the earth warmed at the end of the Ice Age, animals like the oxen and caribou moved north. The families may have followed the animals or adapted to life in a warmer climate.

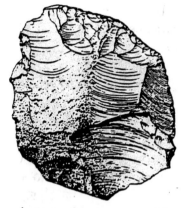

A stone scraper was used by Paleo-Indians to scrape the fur from animal hides.

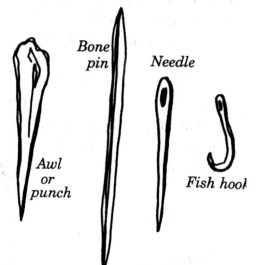

Bone pin

Needle

Awl or punch

Fish hook

ANIMAL BONE TOOLS

The people made tools from animal bones.

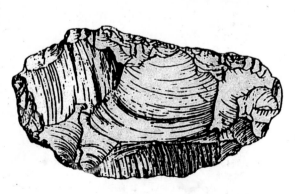

Paleo-Indians cut meat with the edge of this handmade stone knife.

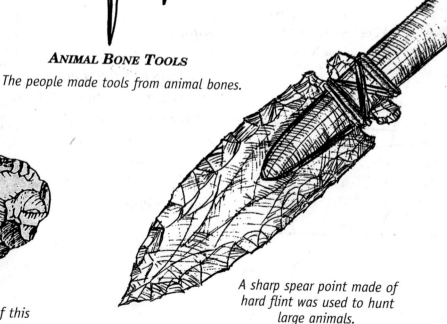

A sharp spear point made of hard flint was used to hunt large animals.

The people used spears to kill mammoths and other large animals for food.

Archaic Indian People

Much later, a new group of people arrived in Ohio. They are called the Archaic Indians. *Archaic* means very old. They lived in Ohio's tall forests. They made stone axes to chop down the small trees. They took bark off large trees so they would die. Then they cut and burned into them until they fell. They made dugout canoes from the thick tree trunks.

The Archaic Indian people were hunters who used spears. At the end of each spear was a sharp spear point made of flint. They developed a hooked spear thrower called an *atlatl*. It could throw spears much farther and faster.

The huge mammoths were gone from the land. The people hunted some of the smaller, faster animals and birds we know today such as deer, wild turkeys, bears, ducks, and geese.

All parts of the animals were

Everything the Archaic people used was made from what they found in nature. This canoe was made by hollowing out a tree trunk.

used. The flesh was used as food. Hides were made into clothing, blankets, moccasins, and bags. Bones and antlers were used for tools. The sinew (strong fibers) was used for sewing. Claws and teeth were sometimes made into necklaces and ornaments.

The people dug for freshwater clams. They made nets to fish in Ohio's many rivers and streams.

Like the Paleo-Indians before them, the Archaic Indian people disappeared from Ohio with barely a trace. If you are ever in one of Ohio's many state parks with trees and rocky cliffs all about you, try to imagine what it must have been like to live as these ancient people did.

The Glacial Kame People

One group of Archaic Indians are called the Glacial Kame people. A *kame* is a small mound of gravel left by retreating glaciers. The Glacial Kame people buried their dead in these gravel mounds.

How Tall?
Archaic men were about five feet and four inches tall. Compare this to men you know.

Children helped gather nuts, berries, and plant roots for food.

The Archaic people made brush shelters to live in. They also lived in caves.

People learned how to make a spear thrower called an atlatl (ATL atl).

33

The Woodland Tradition

A very large group of people soon arrived in Ohio. Like the people before them, they hunted animals and gathered nuts and other wild food. But they did something different. They grew some of their own food and saved it for winter. This meant that they did not have to move so much to find food. They lived in semi-permanent villages along Ohio's rivers and streams. *Semi-permanent* means they lived at least part of the year in these villages. A *permanent* home would be lived in all of the time.

These Woodland people are sometimes called *Mound Builders* because they built large earthen mounds in many shapes. Some looked like animals. The mounds were probably used for religious ceremonies, though no one knows for sure. Some mounds were forts for protection from other groups of people and wild animals. Other mounds were burial sites. Mounds may have been used as places for ceremonies and celebrations.

How did they build the mounds without any modern tools? People used their strong bodies to dig earth in one place and carry it in baskets to the mound site. They probably walked up wooden ramps to pile the earth higher and higher. It must have taken many, many years for thousands of people to build the larger mounds.

Woodland villages were built along the rivers. Why do you think the people built them there?

The Woodland people used the "coil method" of making pottery. You have probably used this way of making a pot by winding a "snake" of rolled clay up into the shape of a pot.

Linking the past and the present

Imagine that you and your classmates are Mound Builders. Make drawings of things that are important in your lives. You can also cut out pictures from magazines or use family photos. Place your pictures in a large box. This box is your mound.

After a month, imagine that hundreds of years have passed. Now pretend that you and your classmates are archaeologists. Open the box and look at the objects one by one. Why were the objects important to the class?

The Adena People

One group of Woodland people are called the Adena. Thousands of Adena mounds have been found. Where did the people live? They chose a site above a river or stream. They needed the water for cooking, drinking, and washing. They also used the rivers for transportation.

Sometimes, especially in winter, some people lived in caves. They could build a fire in the cave and keep warm. At other times they built homes. To make their houses, they dug holes in the ground in a circle. Then they cut down thin trees, took off all the branches, and made tall poles. They placed a pole in each hole. Then they wove branches and grasses onto the pole frame. Sometimes they covered the frames with woven reed mats and animal hides. Family homes were small.

The Adena men and women planted and harvested crops for food down in the rich soil near the rivers. They grew sunflowers, goosefoot, and smartweed. Seeds from pumpkins and squash have been found in Adena caves.

The people worked hard to provide homes, food, and clothing. They were also great artists. They made beautiful objects like the famous Adena pipe. They created fine jewelry and tablets decorated with figures.

The Adena Mounds

The Adena workers built two kinds of mounds. Cone-shaped mounds were used for burial. Some of these mounds were only a few feet high. Usually just one person was buried in them. But other cone-shaped mounds were very large. They were used to bury dead people in many layers.

What was buried in the mounds? Most of the dead were placed in log tombs or basins lined with clay. Their bodies were painted with red or black. Around the bodies were stone pipes, stone tablets engraved with art, and jewelry. The jewelry was made of copper. A few of the dead, however, were *cremated* (burned) and placed in simple graves inside the mounds.

Adena families dug for flint and pipestone, and then traded with other people living in North America. Adena objects have been found as far away as Vermont, Maryland, and Wisconsin!

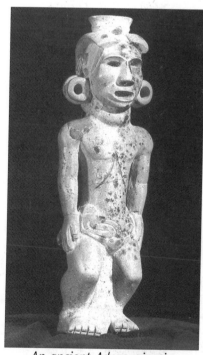

An ancient Adena pipe is over 2,000 years old. Notice the large earrings.

The Miamisburg mound is the largest Adena burial mound. It is sixty-eight feet high. Its base covers more than three square acres.

The Adena people may have built effigy mounds. An *effigy* is an image, or a work of art, in the shape of a living thing. Mounds shaped liked birds, snakes, and other animals have been found throughout Ohio.

We call these people Adena because bones and artifacts were first found on an estate called Adena. It was near Chillicothe. The Adena estate belonged to Thomas Worthington. He was one of Ohio's earliest governors.

Chillicothe

This drawing shows how a mound was made over the graves.

A burial mound looks like this today.

The Great Serpent Mound

The Great Serpent Mound is so unique that it is now a state memorial.
Photo by Tom Till

Great Serpent Mound

The Great Serpent Mound is the most famous mound in Ohio. It is shaped like a curling snake, about to capture an egg in its mouth. It curves more than a thousand feet on a bluff high above Brush Creek. Its tail finally winds three times around in perfect coils.

Few objects have been found inside the Great Serpent Mound. Archaeologists believe this means that the mound was used for religious ceremonies and not burial. Most historians think the Adena built the mound. A few think the Hopewell or Fort Ancient people built it.

Since ancient times, people have been fascinated by snakes. This might be because a snake sheds its skin every year. This makes the snake a symbol of rebirth, or living forever. Maybe the Adena people gathered on this mound on warm summer nights or cold winter ones hoping to live forever.

How was the Great Serpent Mound discovered? After a tornado ripped over the hill and tore down most of the trees, the huge winding mound was seen from another hilltop.

The Hopewell People

No one knows what happened to the Adena. They may have changed their lifestyle or mixed with another group of people. We call the next group who lived here the Hopewell people.

Like the Adena, the Hopewell men and women hunted animals, gathered wild plants, and raised crops. Most of their villages were also in the southern part of today's Ohio. But they also moved northward. They built their villages next to a river or stream.

The mounds of the Hopewell were usually *geometric* in shape. This means they had a form like a circle, rectangle, square, or even an octagon. The modern cities of Marietta, Portsmouth, and Newark are all built on the sites of old Hopewell mounds.

You can visit Circleville today. When pioneer settlers came to this place, they found mounds built by the Hopewells in *concentric* circles. This means circles within circles. The town of Circleville was laid out right in the pattern of the old mounds.

We call these people the Hopewell people because bones and artifacts were first found on the farm of a man named Captain Hopewell.

Ancient Works at Circleville

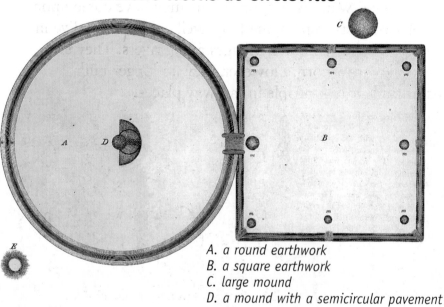

A. a round earthwork
B. a square earthwork
C. large mound
D. a mound with a semicircular pavement
E. dome 90 feet high

This old map shows the way earthworks were formed in some places.

The Hopewell cremated most of their dead. They burned the dead bodies until they were ashes. Mounds were then built over the ashes. Very important people, however, were not cremated. They were buried in their best clothes and jewelry.

The people also built tall earthen walls around large fields. The fields were probably used for religious ceremonies, for gathering a large group of people together, or as a kind of marketplace. Fort Ancient was a huge complex. Its walls were many miles long and three to twenty-three feet high. The walls enclosed stone pavements and mounds. Fort Hill had walls that were nearly twenty feet high. We can only imagine what ceremonies the Hopewell might have performed there.

Trading Near and Far

The Hopewell people traded even more than the Adena people. They used copper from Lake Superior, pearls and seashells from the Gulf of Mexico, and silver from Canada. The people especially loved obsidian, a black volcanic glass. They used it, along with grizzly bear claws, to make jewelry. They traded as far away as the Rocky Mountains for these precious objects!

Sadly, no one knows for certain what became of the Hopewell people. War, disease, or famine may have come upon them. Archaeologists think some Hopewell continued to live in northern Ohio. They still built villages along rivers. They even learned how to grow corn. However, they no longer built mounds or traded with people in faraway places.

This effigy pipe was carved from pipestone.

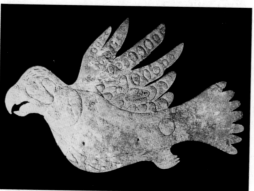

Thin sheets of copper were pressed onto clay figures and used as ornaments or necklaces.

The Hopewell people traded many things, like this obsidian spear point and blades.

On the bank of the Great Miami River in Dayton, volunteers have dug some remains from a Fort Ancient village. Workers have built homes to look just like the ones the people lived in hundreds of years ago. You can visit the Sunwatch site to learn more about the Indians who lived there.

The Late Prehistoric Tradition

When some Woodland people still lived in the north, a new group appeared in the south. The people were part of the Late Prehistoric Tradition. They lived in villages built high above the rivers. They surrounded their villages with log fences called stockades. Their two most important crops were corn and beans.

The Fort Ancient People

The Fort Ancient people are the most important Late Prehistoric group. They lived in today's southern Ohio and Kentucky. They built houses shaped like circles and rectangles. Their houses were placed around an open area at the center of their villages.

At first the Fort Ancient people built burial mounds. Later they buried people in cemeteries with no mounds.

The people are called the Fort Ancient people because they built some of their villages on or near the Fort Ancient site of the Hopewell.

Hunters, Farmers, and Traders

The Fort Ancient people were great hunters of deer, elk, fox, squirrel, and wild turkeys. They were also excellent farmers. They grew corn, beans, and squash. The people learned better ways of farming the rich soil. They made hoes from deer and elk antlers and clam shells. They used the hoes to clear weeds and break up the soil. They made digging sticks to make holes for the seeds.

The Fort Ancient people were great traders. They traded with people in many places. Men and women wore beautifully carved clips in their hair and long strands of beads around their necks. These things came from other places.

This pot is decorated with a duck design.
Photo by Mike Bitsko

Where Did They Go?

Like the other groups, the Fort Ancient people may have left Ohio. They might have been driven out by other tribes who wanted the land for themselves. Many historians believe the Fort Ancient people became the ancestors of the Shawnee tribe.

This is the beginning of a Fort Ancient city. Why do you think the men are building a stockade around the mound?

41

Primary and Secondary Sources

What helps you learn about people of the past? Books? Movies? Photographs? How about spears, pottery, or even bones?

There are two kinds of sources to help us learn what happened a long time ago. We have **primary** sources and **secondary** sources. What is the difference?

Primary sources are made by the people who were there at the time. Primary means "first," or a first-hand account. A Paleo spear point is a primary source. A piece of mammoth bone is a primary source. A burial mound is also a primary source. Can you think of others?

Secondary sources are written, or made to show, something in the past. A book about Mound Builders is a secondary source because the author didn't actually see that little boy practice throwing a spear. The author didn't see the family sleeping peacefully at night around their campfire because it was too long ago.

On a piece of paper, number from 1 to 10. Put a "P" for primary source, or an "S" for secondary source by each item.

1. A movie showing a mammoth hunt
2. A home video your father takes of you learning to ride a bike
3. A stone knife found in an ancient trash pile
4. A diary account by an early explorer, telling about the native people he met
5. An effigy pipe made by the Adena that you see in a museum
6. A model of a wickiup
7. A burial mound
8. Jewelry found in a burial mound
9. Modern paintings of Mound Builder villages
10. This textbook (Look back through the chapter to see pictures of both primary and secondary sources.)

Prehistoric people left no written language. But they did leave drawings and carvings on rock. Is this ancient drawing a primary or a secondary source? What clues might it give you about the person who drew it?

Photo by Tom Till

Activity

How Do You Use the Land?

You may not realize it, but you use land, water, and other natural resources every day. Long ago, children your age also used natural resources, only in different ways. On a piece of paper, label two lists. Write in examples under each list.

Hint: the word "land" means any natural resource.

How Early People Used the Land

1. _____
2. _____
3. _____
4. _____

How I Use the Land

1. _____
2. _____
3. _____
4. _____

Chapter 2 Review

1. Name at least four kinds of artifacts early people left behind.
2. The first group of people who lived here are called the _____ Indians.
3. The second group of people who came here are called the _____ Indians.
4. The Woodland people buried their dead in mounds made of _____.
5. The Adena usually built their villages near a _____.
6. The Ohio mound that looks like a snake is called the _____ _____ Mound.
7. The Hopewell people usually built their mounds in even _____ shapes such as circles, squares, or rectangles.
8. The Hopewell people were great traders. They traveled a long way to trade for _____ from Lake Superior, _____ and _____ from the Gulf of Mexico, and _____ from Canada. They got grizzly bear _____ from the Rocky Mountains.
9. How did the Fort Ancient people get their name?
10. What artistic things could the Fort Ancient people make?

Geography Tie-In

1. Find out if there were any Woodland or Late Prehistoric people who lived near you. Visit an actual site or museum if you can. Get on the Internet, and see if you can find more information about these people. Try **www.OhioHistoryCentral** for the best sites.

2. Ancient people traveled to find animals to hunt for food, and wild plants they could eat. They also traveled during different seasons of the year. What might be some other reasons fathers and mothers took their children to faraway places?

Chapter 3

THE TIME
1600s–1760

PEOPLE TO KNOW
Iroquois
Erie
Wyandot
Miami
Mingo
Ottawa
Shawnee
Delaware

PLACES TO LOCATE
New York Colony
Canada
Sandusky River
Piqua
Maumee River Valley
Chillicothe
Atlantic Coast

Timeline of Events

1600s — Erie Indians live in eastern Ohio.

1650 — Fort Ancient people leave our region.

1655 — The Iroquois destroy the Erie Indian Nation.

1600　　　　1620　　　　1640

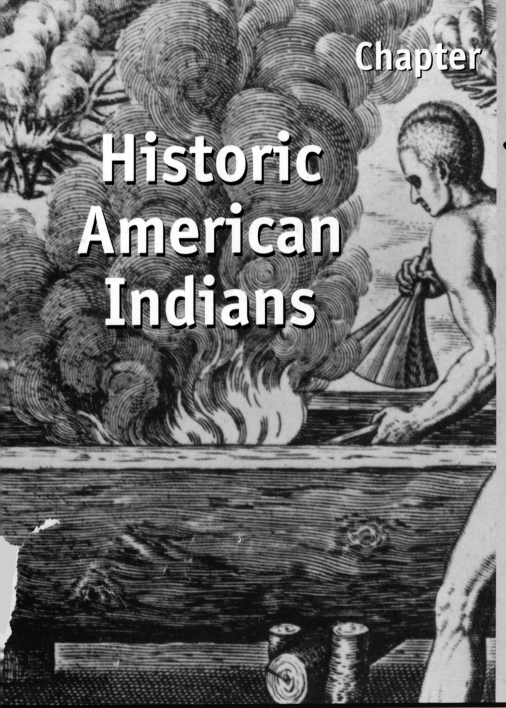

Chapter 3

Historic American Indians

Chapter 3

WORDS TO UNDERSTAND
historic
prehistoric
tepee
wigwam
longhouse
imitate
vision quest
lavish
temporary
shaman
Great Spirit
abundant
confederation
legend

To make a canoe, Americans Indians burned out the center of a large log, scraped out the burned wood, and burned out another layer. What work is each man doing?

1720-1760
Six historic Indian
tribes arrive in Ohio.

| 1680 | 1700 | 1720 | 1740 | 1760 |

Historic Indians

Ohio stood empty of all people for many years. Far away in the New York colony, however, lived a very large group called the Iroquois. They were a nation made up of six tribes. The Iroquois were known as fierce warriors. They bought guns from Dutch and British traders. They hunted and traded animal furs for the guns. The wars went on for many years.

The Iroquois considered the Ohio country their hunting ground. They destroyed whole tribes who stood in their way.

But the Iroquois could not hold back other tribes forever. Many groups wanted to settle in the beautiful country with its animals, rich soil, and many rivers. Six historic tribes of Native Americans came to live in Ohio. Each tribe settled in a specific place. Each lived in peace with the other tribes most of the time. They spread out in a great circle.

Early explorers and settlers wrote in their journals and letters about the Native Americans they met. Because we have a written history about those people, we call them *historic*.

No one living at the time wrote about *prehistoric* people who lived here first. Do you know why?

The beautiful Ohio country was home to many American Indian groups.

Photo by Kathleen Stockwell

Historic Indian Groups

Ottawa

Wyandot

Mingo

Miami

Delaware

Shawnee

46

The Wyandot

The Wyandot may have been the first historic tribe to settle in Ohio. They were also called the Huron. The Iroquois had destroyed many of the Huron in wars in Canada. A small group of them traveled south and settled along the Sandusky River. Their main town was at a place that is now called Upper Sandusky.

The Wyondot were special friends of the Shawnee. They called the Shawnee tribe their "Nephew" or their "Younger Brother." The other Ohio tribes looked up to the Wyandot. They called them the "Grandfathers." They were known as a brave and wise people.

The Miami

The Miami were the next tribe to enter Ohio. They traveled south from Canada. They settled along the rivers that still bear their name. One of their main towns was Pickawilliny, near the present town of Piqua.

The Miami men were brave warriors. They were never known to lose in battle. They wore few clothes and covered their bodies in tattoos.

The Miami women were known as great farmers. They grew a special white corn that had come all the way from Mexico. Their fruit orchards ran for miles along the river valleys.

A group of Miami people prepare a fire.
What clues in the drawing tell you the weather was cold?

The Erie Indians

The Erie Indians lived in many villages in eastern Ohio in the early 1600s. They grew food and hunted.

The Erie and Iroquois were enemies. Both groups were great warriors. There was a terrible war between the two tribes. The bows and poison arrows of the Eries were no match for the guns of the Iroquois.

Other battles with other tribes followed until there were few Erie people left.

The Mingo

The Mingo were a collection of several tribes who followed the Miami into Ohio. Some of the Mingos came from the Seneca tribe. Others came from the Tuscarora tribe. Both tribes were of the Iroquois nation.

Most Mingos settled in the rugged hill country of Ohio. Some came to central Ohio. They had grown tired of the many wars of the Iroquois. They wanted only to hunt and farm in peace. Their main village was usually called Mingo Town.

The Ottawa

The Ottawa came next. They left Canada and headed for the Maumee River Valley. Here they found rich hunting grounds and a river filled with many fish.

Many great warriors came from this tribe, but like the other tribes, they preferred peace and trading to fighting. They were known as the best traders in the Great Lakes region. They were also the only Ohio tribe to live in *tepees*. The other tribes lived in *wigwams* or in *longhouses*.

Leather straps across their foreheads helped women carry heavy loads.

Would you have liked to live in an Ottawa village like this? Other Ohio Indian tribes lived in wigwams or longhouses.

The Shawnee

The Shawnee came from the south and the east. They might be the descendants of the Fort Ancient people who fled from the Iroquois. They returned to their former homeland and fought bravely to keep it.

They were a tall and handsome people. They were brave and respected warriors. The Shawnee were fiercely loyal to the Wyandot Indians and called them the "Uncles."

Tecumseh was a great Shawnee leader. We will read about him in Chapter 5.

The Shawnee called their main town a "chalagatha." The word survives today in the town name of Chillicothe.

The Delaware

The Delaware, also called the Lenape, were the last tribe to settle in Ohio. They came from the east. They were tired of fighting the Iroquois and the American colonists there. They wanted to live in peace in the rugged hill country of Ohio.

The other tribes respected the Delaware for all they had suffered. They called them the "Grandfathers" because they were thought to be from one of the oldest Indian nations.

Johnny Cake

Have you ever eaten "Johnny cake"? It's also called corn bread. Settlers called it "Shawnee cake." They learned to make the bread from the Shawnee and other tribes.

This art shows Delaware people. How do you think the cups on the ends of the long poles might have been used? From the drawing, what tools or weapons did the people use to get food?

49

Daily Life

The life of the people in all the tribes was guided by the seasons. Each season was full of different activities for the people.

- Spring: time to clear fields and plant crops
- Summer: time for hunting and for caring for crops
- Fall: time to harvest crops
- Winter: time for some of the men to leave the villages and spend the winter hunting

The Life of Men and Women

Most American Indian people lived in groups, much like we live in neighborhoods today. Children often lived in the same house as their cousins, aunts, uncles, and grandparents. There were always relatives and friends to play with. They helped each other do all the jobs.

Everyone had a job to do in an Indian tribe. The men watched over their families. They cleared the fields for planting in the spring. They hunted and fished. They defended their villages during war. During the cold winters they kept their families alive by hunting.

Indian women were farmers. They planted corn, beans, and squash in the spring and harvested the crops in the fall. They dried the corn and beans and stored them for winter. They cooked the food over an open fire or in pits in the ground.

The women and girls in a family also prepared the animal skins so they would be soft. When a boy or girl needed a new shirt or new moccasins, it was the women who cut the leather and laced it together with a bone needle. After white settlers came, Indian families often wore clothes made from cloth.

The Life of Children

Indian children learned by *imitating*, or copying, their parents. Small boys were given bows and arrows. The boys played in the fields around the villages. They pretended they were great hunters and warriors just like their fathers and older

The women planted the gardens and cared for them. They often planted squash and beans under the corn.
Photo by Roberta Stockwell

Sunflowers were a source of food.
Photo by Roberta Stockwell

50

brothers. Girls followed their mothers and grandmothers into the fields. By watching the older women, they learned to look after the crops and the younger children. They learned to cook and make clothes for their families.

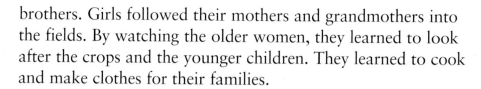

A Vision Quest

Becoming an adult was a special time. When a boy was about thirteen years old, he fasted. This means he took no food or drink for many days. Then he went out into the wilderness all by himself. He waited until he had a dream or vision of an animal or spirit. This journey was called a *vision quest*.

The animal or spirit in the vision would tell the boy something important about his future life. When he returned to his village, tired and hungry, he was no longer a child. He could hunt and fight alongside the older men.

When a girl was about the same age, her family held a great feast for all the village. There were special ceremonies. This celebration told the young men that the girl was now ready for marriage and a family.

What Did They Wear?

Different groups wore different styles of clothes, but when it was cold, they all wore warm leggings, skirts, and robes of animal furs. They used wool blankets, too. Winter moccasins went high up on the leg, while summer moccasins were cut lower.

When the weather was warm, the children often did not wear clothes. Adults wore very little.

The people liked to decorate their clothes. Some used a sash, while others used beads made of bone or shells. Part of the decorating was to paint their skin, too. They sometimes painted their faces, arms, and chests. For special ceremonies, the people decorated themselves more, just like we do today.

Miami men and women liked *lavish* tattoos on their bodies. People in many groups wore ornaments in their pierced noses and ears.

Shawnee men and women loved silver. The men often wore silver medals tied around their necks with brightly colored beads. The women wove silver jewelry into their long black hair.

When it was cold, women wore leather clothing. This woman was dressed up for the photograph in fancier clothes than she wore everyday. She carried her baby on a cradle board.

Moccasins were worn by all the people.

For special occasions and sometimes everyday, men painted their faces and wore a lot of jewelry.

52

Native American Homes

Depending on what tribe they belonged to, the people lived in three main kinds of houses. These were permanent homes. The people lived in them from the spring to the fall.

When they were hunting during the winter months, the men made *temporary* shelters that could be packed up and moved quickly, or just left behind.

A *tepee* is a house made of tall poles with animal skins wrapped around them. The people cooked their food inside the tepee over the fire. The smoke went up and outside an opening in the top. Tepees were fairly warm and very cozy. They could be taken down and moved if the people needed to find a new home. Only the Ottawas lived in tepees in Ohio, but many groups lived in them in other places.

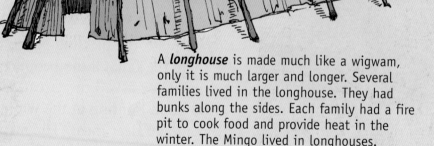

A *longhouse* is made much like a wigwam, only it is much larger and longer. Several families lived in the longhouse. They had bunks along the sides. Each family had a fire pit to cook food and provide heat in the winter. The Mingo lived in longhouses.

A *wigwam* is a house made with a wooden frame covered with tree bark or woven grasses and branches. A fire pit was in the center. The people slept on the ground on blankets of fur. Wigwams were usually clustered near each other in villages. Around the villages were fields of corn. The Miami, Wyandot, Shawnee, and Delaware lived in wigwams.

Spiritual Beliefs

The American Indians all believed in the *Great Spirit*. Some called this Great Spirit the Manitou (MAH-nee-too). The Great Spirit made the world and watched over it with loving care. Other spirits watched over the animals, the plants, the wind, the stars, and the rain.

Every morning Indian men, women, and children prayed to the Great Spirit. They asked the Great Spirit to guide their day. They also prayed before they began any important work like planting, hunting, or going to war.

Shamans told about dreams and visions. They prayed to the Great Spirit and used special rituals and powers to heal the sick.

Dancing for the Great Spirit

The Indian people also prayed to the Great Spirit by dancing. The most important ceremony was the Bread Dance. It was held in the spring and fall. Each tribe did it in their own way.

In the spring, all the people danced in a circle. They beat their drums and sang joyfully. They asked the Great Spirit to give them *abundant* crops. Then they feasted on corn bread and deer meat. The women ate first because their job of farming was so important in the summer. On the next day, they planted their crops with the blessing of the Great Spirit.

In the fall, all the people gathered again. They danced and sang. They asked the Great Spirit for a good harvest in the fall and good hunting in the winter. Then they feasted again on corn bread and deer meat. The men ate first because their job of hunting was most important in the winter. Soon they harvested all their crops and went off to hunt. They believed that they left with the blessing of the Great Spirit.

There were many other Indian dances. The people danced before battle. They danced the Green Corn Dance in early summer when the first corn was ready for picking. They danced in memory of the dead. They also danced just for fun. The young men made a circle. The young women danced in a circle around the men. If a man put out his hand behind him and a young woman took it, this meant they would marry each other!

The Indian people believed in life after death for all creatures. They believed that people, animals, plants, and even the wind and the stars would live forever with the Great Spirit.

Tribal Government

Every Indian village had two leaders. One leader was the village chief. The chief ran the affairs of the village and made important decisions for the people. The chief was usually a man, but there were a few women chiefs.

Each village also had a war chief. The war chief was always a man. He was the bravest warrior in the village. The war chief led the men of the village into battle.

Sometimes all the villages of one tribe would gather in a council. They would talk about their plans and then vote on what to do. Once a vote had been taken, the entire tribe obeyed.

The six Ohio tribes joined together in a *confederation*. This meant they agreed to act together in war and peace.

The rapids of the Maumee River was the most important site for council meetings of all the Ohio tribes. The site is near present-day Maumee.

Before a group went to war, they held a council. The war chief always led the council.

Peace Comes to an End

The six historic tribes loved their new Ohio home. They wished to live here in peace forever. But other people wanted the beautiful country called Ohio, too. Some wanted only to trade with the Ohio Indians. But the American colonists were farmers and wanted to own the land. They wanted the Indians to give or sell all the land to them.

The Indians believed a person could own things such as horses or guns, but not land. They believed that the Great Spirit had given the land to all people to share.

The greatest Ohio chief was a Shawnee named Tecumseh. He told the settlers that the Indians could not sell the land.

Sell a country! Why not sell the air, the great sea, as well as the earth? Did not the Great Spirit make them all for the use of his children?

Legacy of the Ohio Indians

The six tribes gave many things to those who followed. They named the rivers and many other places in Ohio. They taught the settlers how to hunt for deer. They showed them how to make corn bread. But their most important gift was a knowledge of the land.

All the trails into Ohio were laid out by the six historic tribes. Soldiers and settlers followed the Indian trails into Ohio. They used them first as wagon roads. Later, canals, railroads, and highways followed close to the old roads. Most of our modern roads still follow those old trails.

Today, Native Americans get together at a powwow celebration. The children dress up in native costumes, dance, play music, and eat traditional food. The boy on the left is doing a grass dance. His costume recalls gently swaying prairie grass on a windy day.

Legends Tell Stories

Old people were greatly loved by the Indian tribes. They were respected for the wisdom they had gained in their long lives. Often the grandmothers and grandfathers were the ones who spent long hours teaching the children skills they needed to know. The elders, as the old people were called, also told *legends* of the past.

A legend was a story that told a history, or how things came to be. They often answered questions about nature, such as why the owl with glowing yellow eyes stays up at night, or why the moon travels across the starry sky.

Legends were told out loud from memory. They were passed from one generation to the next.

Why the Chipmunk Has Black Stripes

Long ago, the animals had tribes and chiefs just like the people. Porcupine was the chief of all the tribes because nothing could ever get close enough to hurt him.

One night, Porcupine called the animals together. He had a very important matter to talk about. From tree tops and holes in the ground, the animals came.

They built a great fire in the forest and rested around it. Porcupine got up to speak. He looked very worried.

"I cannot decide," he said, "whether we shall have night or daylight all the time."

That started a great argument. They all talked at once. You could not hear what anyone was saying, except Bear. He rumbled in a deep voice, "Always night! Always night! Always night!"

"You can talk all you like," squeaked Chipmunk, "but the light will come whether you want it to or not."

The other animals went on roaring and growling. Chipmunk danced with excitement, shrieking, "The light will come! The light will come!"

Then the sun rose above the tree tops. The fire looked weak and pale. It was daylight.

Silence settled upon the animals.

A shrill voice bragged, "What did I tell you. . . ."

"Grrrr!"

Chipmunk was gone like a flash through the trees, with Bear after him. Chipmunk was so quick that he slipped into a hole in a tree before Bear could catch him. But, just before he disappeared, Bear struck at him with his paw.

After that, there have always been black stripes down the backs of chipmunks.

Activity

Using Indian Language

Here are some words in English and Shawnee. Practice saying simple words and phrases in Shawnee. See if your friends can understand you!

English Word	Shawnee Word	Shawnee Pronunciation
Hello	P'so	PEE-so
Yes	Aughaw	AUH-gahw
No	Matta	MAH-tah
Maybe	Queque	KWEH-kweh
I don't know	Kooqu	KOO-kweh
I don't care	Callapache	cah-lah-PAH-chee
I'm glad	Nowassolepo	now-wah-so-LEE-po
I'm sorry	Wallamelawessalepo	walla-mehla-wehsa-LEH-po
Thank you	Neeaway	nee-YAH-way
Goodbye	Napaukechey	nah-paw-KEH-chay

Chapter 3 Review

1. What large Indian group of fierce warriors came from the New York colony to hunt on Ohio land?
2. Which tribe was killed by the Iroquois?
3. Look at the map on page 46. Name the three tribes that lived closest to your town or city.
4. The Ottawas lived in tepees. What kinds of homes did the other tribes live in?
5. What was the last tribe to settle in Ohio?
6. What were some of the jobs of the men?
7. What were some of the jobs of the women?
8. What were some of the activities of the children?
9. When a boy went by himself and fasted for a spiritual vision, he went on a _____ _____.
10. Native Americans believed in a god called the _____ _____.

Geography Tie-In

How many places near you are named after Native American words or groups? Locate them on a map in your classroom.

Chapter 4

THE TIME
1745 – 1795

PEOPLE TO KNOW
LaSalle
Celeron
George Washington
Pontiac
Chief Logan
Little Turtle
Bluejacket
Tarhe the Crane
Anthony Wayne

PLACES TO LOCATE
France
Canada
Great Britain
Fort Duquesne
Pittsburgh
Point Pleasant
Appalachian Mountains
Gnaddenhutten
Fort Washington
Cincinnati
Fallen Timbers
Greeneville

The Struggle for Ohio

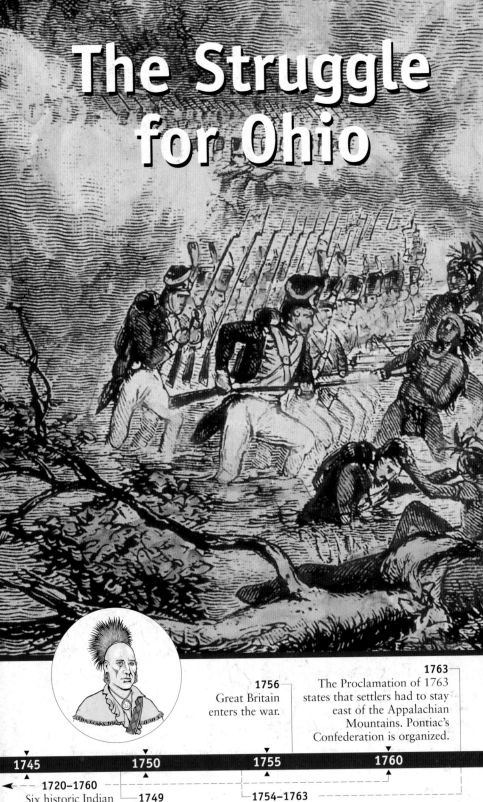

1756
Great Britain enters the war.

1763
The Proclamation of 1763 states that settlers had to stay east of the Appalachian Mountains. Pontiac's Confederation is organized.

Timeline of Events

| 1745 | 1750 | 1755 | 1760 |

1720–1760
Six historic Indian tribes enter Ohio.

1749
Celeron explores Ohio for France.

1754–1763
The French and Indian War

Chapter

4

WORDS TO UNDERSTAND
colony
sea-to-sea clause
plantation
charter
headwaters
treaty
independence
neutral
ordinance
township
ambassadors
annuities
reservation

The Battle of Fallen Timbers was between the Indian tribes and General Anthony Wayne. It was only one of many battles between Ohio's Indians and the new settlers.

Illustration colored by North Wind

1787
Northwest Ordinance

1795
Treaty of Greeneville

1794
Battle of Fallen Timbers

| 1770 | 1775 | 1780 | 1785 | 1790 | 1795 |

1774
Lord Dunmore's War

1776
Declaration of Independence is signed.

1775–1783
American Revolutionary War

1785
Land Ordinance of 1785

1790
Ohio Indians defeat General Harmar's army.

1791
Ohio Indians defeat General Arthur St. Clair's army.

The Beautiful Country

Although the six historic Ohio Indian tribes loved their new home, they could not keep it to themselves forever. The French who lived in Canada also wanted Ohio. So did the people who lived in the *colonies* along the Atlantic Coast.

The French and the Fur Trade

France is a nation on the continent of Europe. French explorers sailed to Canada and claimed it for France. They found the soil poor and the winters cold. But most of the Indians were friendly. Only the Iroquois were unfriendly to the French.

The French traded guns, kettles, blankets, cloth, and tools with the Indian people. The Indians traded beaver, otter, mink, fox, squirrel, and raccoon furs with the French.

The fur trade brought great wealth to the French. They set up trading posts around the Great Lakes and all along the Mississippi River. Detroit, St. Louis, and New Orleans were their most important towns.

The French also sent Catholic priests as missionaries to teach the Indians about their religion. The priests wore long black coats called "cassocks." The Indians called the priests the "black robes." Many Indians became Catholics, including most of the Miami and Wyandot. They usually combined their new religion with their own native customs.

French trappers caught animals and killed them for their thick furs. They shipped the furs back to Europe. They also traded with the Indian people for furs.

Beaver fur was used to make tall felt hats. They were very popular in European cities.

Who Claimed Ohio for France?

The French claimed the beautiful country they named Ohio as part of their empire. They believed that two of their explorers had declared Ohio to be French territory.

• **LaSalle**: This daring young man explored the Mississippi River, then discovered the Ohio River. Later he built the first ship on Lake Erie.

• **Celeron:** He was another brave Frenchman who traveled down the Ohio River. Then he journeyed up the Great Miami and Maumee Rivers. Along his route he buried lead plates in the ground. This was his way of claiming Ohio for France.

LaSalle asks the king of France for permission to explore the Mississippi River in America.

American Colonists Claim Ohio

There were thirteen colonies on the Atlantic Coast. These colonies belonged to Great Britain, another country in Europe. Some of these colonies had *sea-to-sea clauses* in their charters. They believed Ohio belonged to them.

The colony of Virginia had a sea-to-sea clause in its charter. The Virginians grew tobacco, wheat, and corn on large farms called *plantations*. Many people in the colony were slaves who worked on the plantations. Most of the good land along the coast was gone. Many Virginians wanted to set up plantations in Ohio.

A *charter* is a document written when a colony is started. A sea-to-sea clause says that a colony owns all the land from its eastern border to the Pacific Ocean.

The Thirteen Colonies

⊙ **Capital City**
Note: Some colonies had two capital cities. In some states, these are not the current state capitals.

New Hampshire
Portsmouth
New York
Boston
Massachusetts
Hartford ⊙
New Haven ⊙
Providence
Newport
Rhode Island
Connecticut
New York ⊙
Perth Amboy ⊙
Pennsylvania
Burlington
Philadelphia
New Castle
Annapolis ⊙
New Jersey
Delaware
Maryland
Virginia
Williamsburg ⊙
Appalachian Mountains
North Carolina
Atlantic Ocean
New Bern ⊙
South Carolina
Charleston
Georgia
Savannah

N W E S

0 50 100 150
Scale of Miles

French and Indian War

George Washington

George Washington was only twenty-two years old when he first journeyed toward Ohio. He was a tall young Virginian with bright red hair. He was a surveyor by trade. This meant he laid out the boundaries of land. He and his older brother owned land in Ohio. They believed it was a perfect place for all Americans to settle.

Washington went on to become a great soldier. But he never forgot Ohio. When he became the first president of the United States, he sent armies into Ohio to win the country for the United States. He also wanted to build a canal to connect the rivers of Virginia with the rivers of Ohio. He died before this dream could be realized.

Soon a war broke out between the French and the American colonists. They both wanted to control the land and the fur trade. The French built Fort Duquesne (doo-CANE) at the *headwaters* of the Ohio River. The headwaters is the place where a river begins. This is now the city of Pittsburgh. They told the Indians that the Americans must be kept out of Ohio. They said that the colonists would destroy the fur trade for the French. They said the colonists would take all the land away from the Indians.

The Virginians wanted Ohio. They convinced the other twelve colonies to join them in the fight. They all wanted to live in the beautiful country.

The Ohio Indians did not like the Virginians. They called them the "Shemanese." This meant "long knives." Soon they called all the American colonists the Long Knives. Many of the Indians joined the French in the war. They wanted to continue the fur trade. They did not want the Americans to take Ohio away from them.

The Governor of Virginia sent George Washington and some soldiers to the Ohio Valley. Their job was to tell the French that Ohio belonged to Virginia. Fighting broke out between Washington's men and the French. This was the beginning of the French and Indian War.

George Washington was sent to the Ohio River to fight the French and the Indians.

Illustration colored by North Wind Pictures

A Terrible War

The war was very brutal. The French and Indians attacked settlements in Virginia, Pennsylvania, and Kentucky. The Indians often "scalped" their victims. They cut a piece of scalp and hair off of the dead person's head. They did this as a trophy of war. They also believed the dead person could now go back to the Great Spirit.

The American colonists attacked Indian villages throughout Ohio. They killed Indian men, women, and even children. They burned many villages to the ground. They set all the fields of corn, beans, and squash on fire. It was a terrible time for the Indian people of Ohio.

Soldiers finally came from Great Britain to help the American colonists. The Americans called the fight the French and Indian War. The British called the fight the Seven Years War because they fought alongside the Americans for seven years.

At first, the British soldiers lost many battles in the wilderness. They dressed in bright red uniforms. That's why they were called "red coats." They marched in long lines through the woods. The Indians hid behind the trees and gunned down the soldiers. But with the help of the American colonists, the British soldiers won the war.

A Treaty Ends the War

Finally, Great Britain and France signed the first Treaty of Paris. A *treaty* is an agreement made between groups of people. Each group promises to do certain things. France gave all its land in North America to Great Britain. Ohio then belonged to the British.

British means coming from Great Britain. England is part of Great Britain.

Great Britain Rules Ohio

Great Britain wanted to continue the fur trade with the Ohio Indians. But many of the men sent out to deal with the Indians were very cruel. The head of the British soldiers in America was named Jeffrey Amherst. He hated the Indians and called them "beasts." He said that he hoped the Indians would catch smallpox and die.

Pontiac's Revolt

A young Indian named Pontiac wanted to bring the French back to America. He was an Ottawa. He grew up to be a great hunter and warrior.

Pontiac's plan was simple. He would unite all the tribes living around the Great Lakes, including the six Ohio tribes. They would then attack all the British forts and trading posts on the same day. The British soldiers would all be killed. Then the French would return and the Indians would live in peace.

The daring plan almost worked. The Indians captured many forts and trading posts. But Detroit and Pittsburgh held out. The British soldiers fought hard. Many young Indians fighting with Pontiac grew tired. They returned home to help their families during the long winter hunting season. Pontiac was defeated.

Pontiac fled west into Illinois. There he was killed by his own people. They were angry at him for not winning the war.

The Americans Fight for Ohio

The American colonists were also angry at the British. After the French and Indian War, they hoped to settle Ohio. The British said, "No!"

Great Britain passed a law called the Proclamation of 1763. This law drew an imaginary line down the Appalachian Mountains. The British told the American colonists not to cross this line. They wanted the West, including Ohio, to remain Indian hunting grounds. They wanted Ohio for the fur trade and not for farms.

Pontiac

Lord Dunmore's War

Governor Dunmore of Virginia started a war to take Ohio away from the Indians.
The Ohio Indians joined together to stop the colonists. Their leader was a Shawnee chief named Cornstalk. He led the Indians against the Virginians at the Battle of Point Pleasant along the Ohio River. After the battle, Cornstalk signed a treaty with the colonists. He gave Kentucky to the Americans, but Ohio remained with the Indians.

The American Revolution

Do you and your family watch fireworks on the Fourth of July? Most Americans do. They also celebrate with parades and picnics. They are celebrating the day that the thirteen colonies declared their *independence* from Great Britain. Ohio played a part in this great event!

The thirteen colonies were angry at Great Britain for many reasons. Great Britain wanted to control the colonies. It sent governors to most of the colonies. They taxed the people without the approval of their leaders. Tea, glass, lead, and paper were all taxed. Great Britain told the colonies what products they could manufacture. They also told them not to move west into Ohio.

Many leaders in the colonies decided to fight Great Britain. They wanted to start a new government for their own country. Soon a war called the American Revolution began.

The colonies declared their independence from Great Britain. They called their new country the United States of America. George Washington led the Continental Army against the British. The Continental Congress in Philadelphia became the nation's new government.

Leaders in the colonies signed the Declaration of Independence. They wanted to be free of Great Britain's rule.

Many American Indians Fought the Colonists

The Shawnee, Wyandot, and Mingo joined the British in the war against the Americans. They raided American settlements in Kentucky and western Virginia. They killed many people and took many prisoners. They captured many American children and raised them as their own.

The Miami, Ottawa, and Delaware tried to stay **neutral**. This meant they did not take either side in the war.

The Americans sent soldiers into Ohio to attack the tribes. They killed all the Indian men, women, and even children they could find. They attacked villages of the neutral Indians, too.

A Virginian named George Rogers Clark led men against the Shawnee. In southern Ohio, they burned many Shawnee villages to the ground. Clark and his men went on to capture most of the British forts in the West.

George Rogers Clark fought the British and the Shawnee.

The Logan Elm

Chief Logan was a Mingo who lived in eastern Ohio. The Americans blamed him for attacks on their towns, but he was not responsible. A man named Colonel Cresap did not believe him. He killed Logan's entire family.

Chief Logan stood under an elm tree. He gave a famous speech about his sadness. His speech was so beautiful that American school children often learned it by heart. Here is part of what Chief Logan said:

> *I appeal to any white man to say if he ever entered Logan's cabin hungry and he gave him not meat; if he ever came cold and naked, he clothed him not. . . . One man last spring, in cold blood [for no reason], murdered all the relatives of Logan, not even sparing his wives and children . . . There runs not a drop of my blood in any living creature. . . . Who is there to mourn for Logan? No one.*

The Gnaddenhutten Massacre

A terrible massacre occurred at a Christian Indian mission called Gnaddenhutten (na-den-HUT-ten) on the Tuscawaras River. A massacre means many people are killed. Usually the people do not have any weapons.

David Zeisberger taught many of the Delaware Indians about Christianity. He belonged to a sect called the Moravians. They came from a place in Europe called Moravia. They believed all war was wrong. They also prayed a great deal. They lived together in small villages where everyone helped one another.

The young minister converted many Delaware Indians to his religion. They became known as the Moravian Indians. Zeisberger set up villages for them in eastern Ohio. They lived in peace and refused to fight the Americans.

The Moravians came on sailing ships from Europe. They converted some of the Delaware people to Christianity. Some moved to Ohio to start a religious community.

This did not matter to the Americans. They believed all the Ohio Indians were dangerous. They burned most of the Moravian Indian villages to the ground. At Gnaddenhutten, they met 150 peaceful Indians harvesting their corn. They killed all the Indians without mercy. Only two little boys escaped.

Treaty of Paris, 1783

Even with the help of many Ohio Indians, the British could not defeat the Americans. They signed a peace treaty after eight years of fighting. Great Britain recognized the United States as a free and independent nation. They also gave the United States all the land south of Canada and north of Florida to the Mississippi River. This meant Ohio now belonged to the Americans.

An Ohio Township

6	5	4	3	2	1
7	8	9	10	11	12
18	17	16	15	14	13
19	20	21	22	23	24
30	29	28	27	26	25
31	32	33	34	35	36

← 6 miles →

Each section was 640 acres, or one mile square.

The Land Ordinance of 1785

An **ordinance** is another name for a law. This law divided Ohio into **townships**.
• Each township was six miles square.
• Each township was divided into 36 sections.
• Each section contained 640 acres.

You needed at least $640 to buy a section of land in Ohio. This was only $1 an acre.

Section 16 was always set aside for schools.

The Future of Ohio

Americans were overjoyed that they had won their independence! They were also happy as they looked west to Ohio. The beautiful land could now become a state. But how would this happen? This was the first problem the young nation faced. The plan was simple.

• First, the land must be divided into townships and sold.
• Second, state governments must be established.
• Third, the Indian tribes must surrender their claims to Ohio.

The Northwest Territory

The Northwest Ordinance of 1787

All the land north of the Ohio River and west to the Mississippi River was called the Northwest Territory. Ohio was part of this territory. Parts of the territory would become states in three stages.

First, a governor and three judges would run the territory. Then, when 5,000 free men lived there, the territory could set up a legislature. They could send one representative to the United States Congress. The representative could talk there, but he could not vote. Slavery would be outlawed.

When 60,000 free people lived in the territory, it could become a state.

Treaties with the Indians

There was one major problem with the dreams of the Americans. The Indians were already living in Ohio. If the settlers moved in, what would happen to the Indian people?

George Washington was the first president of the United States. He had fought Indians as a young man. He knew they were good soldiers. He did not want to start a war with them in Ohio. The American people were tired of fighting. The nation also had no army. The soldiers had all gone home to their farms and towns after the American Revolution ended.

The president decided to send *ambassadors* to the Ohio tribes. They met the Indians along the rapids of the Maumee River. They asked the Indians to sign treaties with the United States. The tribes would give up all claims to Ohio. In return, they would receive *annuities*. These were yearly payments of food, money, blankets, and other things the Indians needed. The annuities would be a great deal of money for the time. But they would be pennies compared to the value of the land they were giving up.

> "We all belong to one family . . . we are all children of the Great Spirit . . . we walk in the same path . . . we are friends . . . we must assist each other to bear our burdens."
>
> —Shawnee Chief Tecumseh

What do you think?

What if someone came to your house and told you to sell everything you owned and move away? How would you feel? Try to imagine how the six Ohio tribes felt when they met with Washington's men along the rapids of the Maumee River.

Treaties were signed at a place like this on the Maumee River.
Photo by Roberta Stockwell

Indian Confederation

Three chiefs formed the six Ohio tribes into a confederation. All the young Indian warriors were ready to defend Ohio. They told the ambassadors to go back to Washington with this warning:

Great Father, do not cross the Ohio River with your soldiers! It will run red with the blood of your young men!

Who were the three chiefs who led the Ohio Indians? They were all remarkable men. Each one was respected by his own tribe and all the other Ohio Indians.

• **Little Turtle:** He was the main chief of the Miami. He was known for his intelligence. He was also considered a great warrior. He loved peace, but was bold in battle.

• **Bluejacket:** This Shawnee war chief was actually a white Virginian. His English name was Marmaduke. As a teenager, he had been captured and adopted by the Shawnee. He was wearing a blue shirt the day he was taken. He soon became known as the greatest warrior of his tribe.

• **Tarhe the Crane:** He was called the wisest chief in Ohio. He was named the "Crane" after the many birds that lived in the wetlands near his home along the Sandusky River. He made all the final decisions for the tribes.

The Ohio Indian Wars

President Washington and the American people wanted Ohio as a state. People needed to buy land there. Many Americans hoped for a better life across the Ohio River. People in countries as far away as England, Scotland, Ireland, and Germany also wanted the opportunity for a better life in the rich Ohio farmland. Ohio was called the gateway to the West and to a better life.

Two American armies were sent into Ohio to defeat the Indians. General Josiah Harmar led the first army. His soldiers were young men with little training. Many had not been able to find work or buy land. They joined the army for the pay—two dollars a month. The Ohio Indians easily defeated this army.

A year later, General Arthur St. Clair led another army into Ohio. His soldiers had less training than Harmar's army. Most had no experience in fighting. Some of them brought their wives along with them. The women did the cooking and cleaning for the men.

On a snowy November morning, the Indians attacked the army deep in the woods. Nearly all the American men and women were killed. Only a few people made it back to Fort Washington, the army post at Cincinnati.

"The attack began about a half hour before sunrise. For about five minutes, the Indians yelled . . . the sound was like horse bells ringing all about us . . . then they dashed into our camp. Soon we were completely surrounded!"

—A young soldier describes the attack of the Indians on the army of St. Clair.

The Black Snake

The Indians rejoiced. Surely no other soldiers would try to take Ohio away from them. But President Washington decided to send another general named Anthony Wayne into Ohio. He brought a new group of soldiers.

Wayne was so dedicated that his own men called him "Mad Anthony Wayne." The Indians called him the "Black Snake Who Never Sleeps." Wayne took two years to train his men to fight. He taught them to ride their horses at top speed. He taught them to take deadly aim with their guns. Most importantly, he taught them not to be afraid to fight the fierce Indians.

Indian villages were destroyed during and after the war.

It's hard to believe that this peaceful place was the site of the terrible Battle of Fallen Timbers. It was the final large battle with the Indians in Ohio.

Photo by Roberta Stockwell

The Battle of Fallen Timbers

Anthony Wayne's army was finally ready to fight. He marched his men all the way from Cincinnati to the rapids of the Maumee River. The warriors of Little Turtle, Tarhe the Crane, and Bluejacket were hiding there behind fallen trees that a tornado had knocked down. The fight between the two armies became known as the Battle of Fallen Timbers.

After only one hour of fighting, the Indians ran from the battlefield. They were no match for the highly trained soldiers. The Americans celebrated when they heard the news of the victory along the Maumee River. Now Ohio could be opened for settlement.

Chapter 5

WORDS TO UNDERSTAND
emigrate
fort
pioneer
local
county
state capital
orator
retreat

Families left their homes and came to Ohio by covered wagon. They often traveled in winter because it was easier to travel over the snow and ice.
Art by Glen Hopkinsen

1803
Ohio becomes a state.

1805
Tecumseh and the Prophet organize their confederation.

1813
Seiges of Fort Meigs and Fort Stephenson, and Battle of Lake Erie. Tecumseh dies.

1814
Treaty of Ghent ends the War of 1812 (signed Christmas Eve).

1800

1810

1820

1799
The second stage of territorial government begins.

1811
Battle of Tippecanoe

War of 1812
between the United States and Great Britain.

1815
Battle of New Orleans is fought on New Year's Day (last battle of the War of 1812).

West to Ohio!

Many people wanted to settle in Ohio after the American Revolution ended. Most of them were farmers. They knew the soil of Ohio was rich and fertile. Ohio had many trees for building homes, barns, and fences. Wild animals lived in the forests and fish swam in the rivers and lakes. There was plenty of rainfall. There were many rivers and Indian trails to carry farm goods to market. Ohio would truly be a wonderful place to start a new life!

Who Wanted to Come to Ohio?

Many people from New England wanted to move west. They moved from the New England states of Massachusetts, Connecticut, New Hampshire, and Rhode Island.

Colonists had lived in New England for nearly 200 years. The best land there was already settled. The poor land that remained had rocky soil. Good farms were very expensive to buy. This meant that many families wanted to go to Ohio and

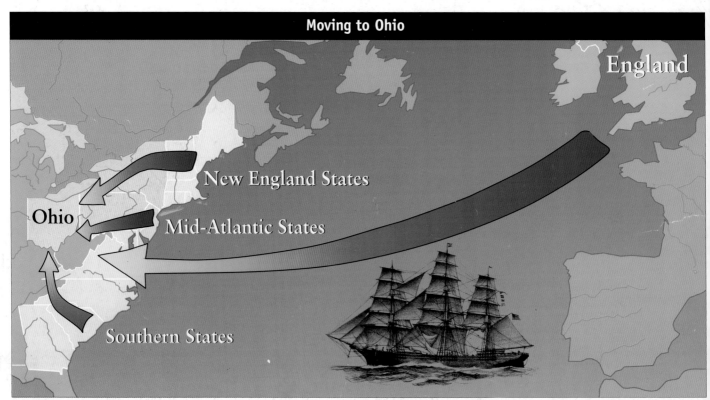

Moving to Ohio

People moved to Ohio from the older states and from England.

start farms in the new land.

The Mid-Atlantic states are New York, New Jersey, Pennsylvania, and Delaware. Good land was expensive there. The promise of farmland at only one or two dollars an acre led many people west.

People from the Southern states also wanted to settle in Ohio. These states are Virginia, Maryland, North Carolina, South Carolina, and Georgia. The wealthiest people owned the best land in these states. Their slaves worked the land. Many poorer people hoped they could buy small farms in Ohio. Many slaves also dreamed of freedom north of the Ohio River.

Once the American Revolution ended, many people from Great Britain also hoped to emigrate to America. *Emigrate* means to leave your home country and move to another one. They traveled on ships across the Atlantic Ocean and then went by land or river routes to Ohio.

What do you think?

Can you imagine leaving your hometown and building a new home someplace else? If you were a pioneer coming to Ohio, what would you take with you? What would you do when you arrived in Ohio?

Activity

Solve a Problem

You have just read that many of the people in the states along the Atlantic Ocean had a hard time getting enough good farmland.

Pretend your family lives in pioneer times. Your father's friend rides up on his horse and stays for dinner. While he is eating potatoes and deer meat your mother has cooked, he tells the family about the rich soil, sunshine, summer rains, and wild animals in Ohio. You all listen to the adventures he had in Ohio.

Late at night, after you and the other children are all asleep, your father and mother talk about making a change in their lives. Your father says the family needs to grow more crops on a larger farm. Your mother thinks the children would feel sad leaving their friends and home behind. Both parents know it will be hard to decide which food, furniture, and clothes to take. A covered wagon doesn't have much room inside. The trip might be long and even dangerous. Could the family cow and dog come along?

Now it's your turn. Work with a friend and use the list below to decide how to make life better for your family. Would you move to Ohio, or would you decide to do something else?

Here are some ways people solve problems or make decisions about what to do:

- State the problem.
- Gather information.
- List many ways to solve the problem.

Think about the good and the bad of each way on the list. Make a decision. It might be hard! How will you know if the decision was a good one?

Fact and Opinion

Facts are things that can be proven to be true, such as "The capital of Ohio is Columbus."

An **opinion** is something that a person thinks is true. "Settlers from England were the best farmers," is an opinion. Another person might think, "Settlers from France were the best."

If something is a fact, you can trust that it is true. If something is an opinion, it is good to find other opinions to get a better idea of the truth. Look at the sentences below. Work with a partner to decide which are facts and which are opinions. Then, when you read this chapter, decide if what you are reading can be proven as fact.

1. Snow falls to the ground.
2. I don't think it will snow today.
3. Mountains are pretty.
4. Ohio has some mountains.
5. Most of Ohio's early settlers were farmers.
6. Ohio had many trees for building homes, barns, and fences.
7. The worst wild animals in Ohio were wolves.
8. The settlers loved living in Ohio.

Research to Get Information

What if you read something in this book that you think is a fact, but you are not sure? There are many ways to get information. It's like a treasure hunt. It's fun! Start by thinking about these sources of information and what you can learn from each one:

- an atlas (maps)
- an encyclopedia (a lot of different information on important topics)
- a dictionary (words and their meanings, and how to say them)
- newspapers (stories written about what is going on right now)
- books (about all subjects)
- Internet (all kinds of information)

As you research, keep notes. Write down where you found the information. You might write something like this:

fort
1. a strong place
2. a place surrounded by an earth wall or strong log fence. (Webster's Dictionary)

Now choose a subject in this chapter, research, take notes, and report what you find.

Connecticut settlers enter the Western Reserve.
Illustration colored by North Wind Pictures

Settling Towns

The first American settlers who came to Ohio were soldiers. They built forts. A *fort* is a large area enclosed by a wooden stockade. Forts were usually built along a river. The soldiers in the fort were supposed to keep the peace between the Indians and the settlers.

When people came to Ohio, they usually wanted to settle near a fort. If the Indians attacked, they would be protected. The settlers could run to the fort and close the gates behind them.

As peace came to Ohio, the soldiers left and the forts were abandoned. The settlers tore down the wooden posts of the fort and used them to build homes.

People also wanted to settle along a river. This made it easy for settlers to come to a new town by boat. Crops and other goods could be sent easily to market down a river. It was harder to take a heavy wagon across the land.

Marietta

Marietta was the first town settled in Ohio. A man named Rufus Putnam brought people from New England down the Ohio River by boat. They built their town near a fort where the Muskingum River meets the Ohio River.

They found many Indian mounds in the area. They respected the ancient mounds, and built their own town cemetery around the biggest one. They turned an ancient Indian trail into their main road. The settlers also built a new fort in the center of town.

The settlers chose the name Marietta for their town. This was in honor of Queen Marie Antoinette of France. The settlers were grateful to the French for their help in the American Revolution.

Marietta, on the Ohio River, was simply a few cabins around a fort. This was Marietta about 1790.

More Ohio Towns

More people founded towns along Ohio's many rivers. Settlers laid out Cincinnati, Steubenville, and North Bend on the Ohio River. Soon people moved up the many rivers that emptied into the Ohio. They founded Dayton on the Miami River, Chillicothe on the Scioto River, and Franklinton (later renamed Columbus) on the Olentangy River. People next settled along Lake Erie. Cleveland was founded on the Cuyahoga River.

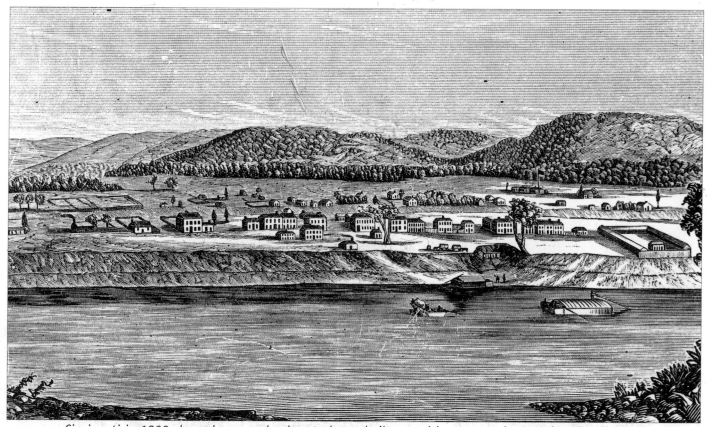

Cincinnati in 1802 shows how people almost always built new cities next to rivers. What river is this?

A French Town on the Ohio River

Some people who came to Ohio did not understand how hard it would be. They thought beautiful towns with homes, stores, and tree-lined streets would be waiting for them. One group of people in France were shopkeepers and artisans. Some grew grapes and made wine from them there. People told them beautiful towns were waiting for them along the Ohio River.

The French arrived in a town called Gallipolis (GAL-la-poh-leese). This means "City of the French" in Latin. They were shocked to find only a clearing in the forest. There were a few wooden huts to live in, but no homes or shops. Many of the people returned to France. Some stayed in Gallipolis. Others went down the river to the French Grants where they started farms.

Ohio's First Cities

Cleveland

Columbus   Steubenville

Dayton   Chillicothe   Marietta

Cincinnati

Gallipolis

Starting Farms

Families usually laid out their farms near a town. Everyone had a job to do on a family farm in pioneer Ohio. A *pioneer* is someone who is the first to do something.

Pioneer Fathers

The father of the family bought the land. He staked out the boundaries of the farm. Then he began the hard job of clearing the trees. This job could take his whole lifetime.

Next he built a small cabin for his family. Later, he built a small barn for the animals and a fence around a pasture.

The farmer used a team of oxen or horses and a plow to turn up the soil. Wheat and corn were the most important crops. Wheat was harvested around the Fourth of July. Corn was harvested in the fall. The farmer also planted fruit orchards. Apples, peaches, and cherries were the favorite fruits.

Pioneer Mothers

The mother in a pioneer family also had much hard work to do. She cooked the meals in the cabin's fireplace. She sewed all the clothes for her family. She also kept a small "kitchen garden" near the cabin. Here she planted vegetables and herbs used for cooking and making medicine. She took care of the children and the older relatives. If there were no schools near the farm, she often taught her children how to read and write.

Pioneer women made soap, dipped candles, and made wool into clothes. At harvest time, they often helped the men in the fields.

The women cooked food in a fireplace.

Women and children made candles from animal fat called tallow.

Pioneer Children

Even children had important jobs to do on the farm. They collected small branches and twigs for the fire in the cabin. They helped their fathers in the fields and orchards. They helped their mothers in the kitchen gardens. They were usually in charge of milking the cows. They also took the cows out to pasture by day and brought them back into the barn at night.

If there was a school nearby, children could usually go only during the winter when they were not needed on the farm.

Children also went on errands for their parents. Sometimes this meant they traveled many miles all by themselves. Read this story of William, a nine-year-old boy. He lived on a farm near Steubenville with his family. William and his horse named Paddy had to take the wheat to town for milling.

Women and girls spun the wool fibers into thread. Then they wove the threads into cloth.
Photo taken at Historic Sauder Village

Father bought a black pony, bearing the name of Paddy . . . . for going to the mill. He would carry three bushels of wheat and me on the top of it, or as many of the children as we could pile on.

It fell to my lot to go to distant mills to get grinding done, and Paddy and I made many a mile of travel. At the mills, we had to wait our turn. . . . Often we would have to leave our wheat, and go after it another day. . . . The weather was fine, the roads were good, there were plenty of apples in the orchards and nuts in the woods by the way. They were always free to the passer-by!

Everyone had to work chopping wood, building a cabin, and cooking food.
Illustration colored by North Wind Pictures

William Henry Harrison

When William Henry Harrison was a little boy growing up in Virginia, everyone called him by his nickname, "Billy." He was the baby in a family of fifteen children. Billy liked to play in the fields near his family's house. He pretended he was a soldier.

When he was eighteen, Billy's family sent him away to school. They wanted him to be a doctor. But Billy still dreamed of being a soldier! He ran away to Ohio and joined the army. He fought beside Anthony Wayne at the Battle of Fallen Timbers. He also defeated the Indians at the Battle of Tippecanoe.

Harrison lived with his wife and children on a farm at North Bend, overlooking the Ohio River. He was the first man from Ohio to become president of the United States.

Ohio Becomes a State

The many people who came to Ohio worked hard to set up local government and state government. *Local* government is the government that is closest to home. (To learn even more about our government, read Chapter 13 in this book.)

Local Government

• **Townships:** In each township, the people met to talk about problems. Then the people voted on what to do.

• **Cities:** The people elected a mayor to run the city.

• **Counties:** Ohio was divided into eighty-eight counties. A *county* is a kind of local government that the colonists brought from England. Every county had courts and a county sheriff.

Stages of Government

• First Stage (1787): General Arthur St. Clair became the first governor of the Territory of Ohio. He and three judges made all the laws for Ohio.

• Second Stage (1799): Soon there were 5,000 free men in Ohio. They elected a state legislature. Many people who came to Ohio from the South wanted to bring their slaves with them. The legislature said, "No!" In Ohio, all people would be free!

They also sent a representative to the United States Congress. His name was William Henry Harrison. When he was in Congress, Harrison wrote and passed an important land law. He said people could pay a small amount when they purchased land. They could then pay off the rest over the next four years.

• Third Stage (1803): Soon more than 60,000 free people lived in Ohio. The people wrote their own state constitution. On March 1, 1803, Ohio became the seventeenth state.

Our Traveling State Capital

The capital city is where the representatives of the state government meet. The first *state capital* was in Chillicothe. It was moved to Zanesville, then back to Chillicothe. Finally, the people decided that a new capital should be built near the center of the state. They called it Columbus.

Old State House, Chillicothe

The Ohio Indians

The year 1803 was a happy one for most Ohioans. They were now part of the United States. Towns and farms were being settled. People were coming from all over to live in their state. The future looked bright.

But not everyone was happy. The Indians were very sad. The Shawnee, Delaware, and Mingo had lost all of their land in the Treaty of Greeneville. The Miami, Ottawa, and Wyandot feared they would soon lose their land too.

The Indians watched as the settlers changed the land. They cut down the trees. They cleared fields for towns and farms. Soon many wild animals disappeared. The buffalo went west. Many of the beaver, fox, and squirrels were killed. Even the white-tailed deer were no longer plentiful.

Without land, the Indians could not grow corn, beans, and squash. Without wild animals, they could not hunt for meat to eat. They had no fur to trade for guns and other goods.

The Indian way of life began to disappear from Ohio. Many chiefs sold the land near their villages to the Americans. Soon whole villages were deserted. Some Indians went west while others struggled to stay in Ohio.

"What will become of my poor Indians?"

—Shawnee Chief Tecumseh

Many Indians became very sick, and thousands died. They caught diseases like smallpox and measles from the settlers. Some Indians started to drink the white man's whiskey. They became alcoholics and no longer took care of their families.

Two Shawnee Brothers

Two Shawnee brothers decided something must be done to save the Indians. First they would unite all the tribes. Then they would win a home in Ohio for their people. The older Shawnee brother was named Tecumseh. He was born along the Mad River near Dayton. His father and most of his brothers had been killed by the Americans.

Tecumseh became a great hunter and warrior. He was the scout of Bluejacket, the Shawnee war chief. He fought at the Battle of Fallen Timbers. He was one of the last men to leave the battlefield.

Tecumseh never accepted the defeat of the Ohio tribes. He spent many years trying to find a way to save his people. He decided to form a confederation of all the Indian tribes. He would teach them that they were one people. He would also teach them that the Indians owned all the land in common. No one tribe could sell any land without an agreement from all the Indians.

Once Tecumseh had united all the tribes, he would tell the Americans to leave Ohio and all the western country. He hoped the Americans would leave peacefully. If they did not, there would be a war. Tecumseh and his warriors would push the Americans out of Ohio. Then it would become the center of a great Indian nation!

Tecumseh traveled throughout America. He convinced many tribes to join his confederation. He was known as a great *orator*. This means he gave speeches that moved people deeply. Here is part of a speech he gave to the Osage tribe.

> *Brothers, we must be united. We must smoke the same pipe. We must fight each other's battles, and more than anything else, we must love the Great Spirit. He is for us . . . he will make his red children happy.*

The War Ends

Many other battles were fought during the War of 1812. The British attacked the American capital at Washington, D.C. They burned the White House where the president lived.

The war ended after nearly three years of fighting. The British promised to respect American independence. No mention was made of an Indian nation in Ohio. The British believed there could be no Indian nation without Tecumseh.

The settlers rejoiced when the war was over. They set off firecrackers and built bonfires to celebrate. They danced and sang long into the night.

Only the Indians remained sad. Their great leader Tecumseh was dead. His confederation had ended in failure.

Chapter 5 Review

1. How were most of the settlers who came to Ohio after the American Revolution planning to earn a living?
2. Which government group divided up Ohio's land for settlement?
3. American soldiers came into Ohio and built _____ along the rivers.
4. What was the first town settled in Ohio? What were some of the other towns?
5. What were the jobs of pioneer men?
6. What were the jobs of pioneer women?
7. What did the pioneer children do on a farm?
8. What were the three kinds of local government in Ohio?
9. Where was the first state capital located? Where is it today?
10. Who became the first United States president from Ohio?
11. What were some ways the lives of the Indians changed after Ohio became a state?
12. What did Tecumseh and the Prophet hope to do for their people?
13. What was the name of the war where the British and Ohio Indians fought the Americans?
14. What caused the death of Tecumseh?

Geography Tie-In

On page 82, look at the map of the many different settlement areas in Ohio. Compare that map to a modern map of Ohio. Can you tell what region you live in? If you had lived then, would your property have been free?

Chapter 6

THE TIME
1815–1860

PEOPLE TO KNOW
Mike Fink
William Dean Howells
William McGuffey
Johnny Appleseed
Shakers
Amish
President Andrew Jackson

PLACES TO LOCATE
Zane's Trace
National Road
Miami and Erie Canal
Ohio and Erie Canal
Ireland
Germany
Switzerland

The Gateway State

Timeline of Events

1811
The first steamboat sails
on the Ohio River.

1815
The "Great Migration"
into Ohio begins.

1818
The National Road reaches the
Ohio River in western Virginia.
The first steamboat sails on Lake
Erie.

1825
Ohio begins
building canals.

1830
Indian Remova
Act becomes la

1815   1820   1825   1830

96

Chapter 6

WORDS TO UNDERSTAND
flatboat
keelboat
sailboat
steamboat
canal
lock
railroad
immigrant
Irish
German
public school
grade school
high school
elementary
parochial school
communal

The Coming Train, painted by Edward Lamson Henry in 1880, shows what it was like to pull up a buggy to greet visitors who arrived by train.

[1]833
National Road reaches [Col]umbus.
[Obe]rlin College is founded.

1837
Oberlin College admits female students.

1840
The National Road reaches the Indiana border.

1843
The last Indians leave Ohio. They don't return for many years.

| [1]835 | 1840 | 1845 | 1850 | 1855 | 1860 |

1835
Oberlin College admits African American students.

1836
Ohio's first railroad is built between Toledo and Michigan.
The first *McGuffey Reader* is published.

1845
The Irish Potato Famine begins.

97

The Gateway State

After the War of 1812, more people moved to Ohio than ever before. So many settlers came that people called it the "Great Migration." Listen to this man from Great Britain who traveled to Ohio during the Great Migration:

Old America seems to be breaking up and moving westward. . . . As we travel to Ohio, we are never out of sight of family groups. . . . They travel before us and behind us night and day!

People then called Ohio the "Gateway State." It truly was the gateway to the West. If you traveled from an eastern state, you usually passed through Ohio on your way west. But Ohio was also the gateway to a better life for many people who settled here.

Flatboats were steered by long poles. They floated down the river.

The Transportation Revolution

With so many people moving to the state, transportation became very important. For a long time, people had been traveling by canoe down the rivers or by foot along the old Indian trails. Now they needed faster ways to travel into Ohio and take farm goods to market out of Ohio.

The people of Ohio started the Transportation Revolution. They came up with better and faster ways to travel in and out of the state.

Flatboats, Keelboats, and Sailboats

The easiest way to get to Ohio was by flatboat. A *flatboat* was a large wooden raft with a small cabin. Flatboats were usually built near the headwaters of the Ohio River. People then floated down the Ohio along with all their possessions. When they arrived at their destination, they broke the boat apart and used it for firewood or lumber for building.

Keelboats could float downriver or be pulled upriver by horses or mules walking along the bank.

A *keelboat* was a round-bottomed boat with the front curved into a point. A wooden keel, or wedge, ran along the bottom. The keel allowed a captain to steer the boat more easily.

A *sailboat* was a keelboat with sails. The canvas sails caught the wind and pushed the ship along.

These boats brought many of the first settlers to Ohio. They also took farm goods down the Ohio River to the Mississippi River. But the boats had many problems. They were very slow. The boats could not go up the river against the current. Many farmers took their crops by flatboat all the way to New Orleans. There they sold the crops and the boat, and walked back to Ohio!

Sailboats were pushed along the water by the wind.

Settlers floated on flatboats to Ohio.
Illustration colored by North Wind Pictures

Mike Fink

The men who guided boats through Ohio's wilderness were often wild themselves. The most famous captain was named Mike Fink. He could shoot a gun better than anybody. He drank and smoked a lot. He had a hot temper and got into many fights. But nobody could steer a boat down the river more safely than Mike Fink.

When the Ohio River became too crowded with boats of all kinds, he headed west for the Mississippi River. People tell stories about him to this day.

99

Steamboats

The steamboat was invented to make travel by water faster and to go in two directions. A *steamboat* has a large paddle wheel. A steam engine turns the paddle wheel and makes the ship go fast! A steamboat can go up or down a river. It does not have to go the way the river flows.

The *New Orleans* was the first steamboat on the Ohio River. The *Walk-in-the-Water* was the first steamboat on Lake Erie.

Many people were afraid when they heard the puffing engines and the whirling paddle wheels of the steamboats in the distance. Some said, "A war has started!" Others said, "It's a thunderstorm coming our way!" A few people even thought the world was ending.

Soon hundreds of steamboats were going up and down the Ohio River and along the Lake Erie shore. The line of steamboats ran for more than a mile along the docks at Cincinnati. The boats took people from town to town. They carried bushels of wheat, corn, and apples to market. They even brought traveling actors and musicians to Ohio.

Steamboats had a steam engine that turned a paddle wheel. They were used to carry goods and people on America's rivers.

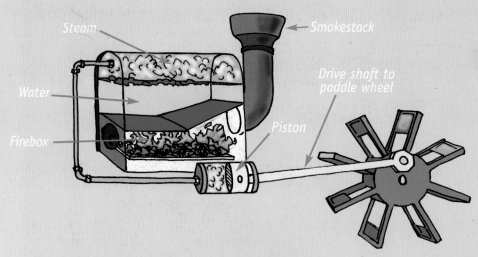

To run a steam engine, men built a large fire under a boiler of water. When the water boiled, the steam pushed against the piston and made it turn the paddle wheel. Sometimes too much steam caused a terrible explosion.

Ohio Builds Roads

The people of Ohio widened the old Indian trails through the woods. Then they placed wooden planks or crushed stone along the trails. This made travel through the woods much easier.

Zane's Trace was the most famous early trail. The trail was wide enough for a person to travel on horseback. Zane and his crew also built ferries to help people cross rivers.

The National Road

The United States Congress decided to build the National Road. The road would start in Maryland. It would run all the way to Vandalia, Illinois.

It took hard work to build the National Road. Men usually laid down ten miles at a time. One crew would clear the forest. Another would carve out the path of the road and lay crushed stones on it. Still another crew would build bridges over the rivers.

Would you have liked to travel down the old National Road? Maybe you can answer this question better after you read what this man saw:

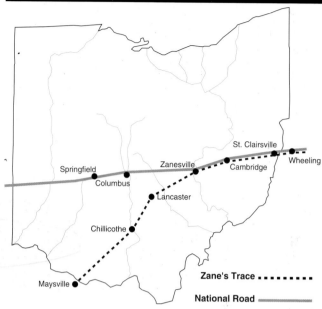

Zane's Trace and the National Road

The National Road became US Highway 40. Does it pass through your town?

Zane's Trace ·········
National Road ————

A one-horse wagon carries a family and all their possessions. Sometimes there are as many as twelve people in a family . . . the littlest ones and the sick ride in the wagon. The father walks by the side of the horse, cheering and encouraging him on the way. . . . The woman walks by her husband or leads a weary child by the hand. She urges the older children to hurry along. The family dog brings up the rear!

Inns for Travelers

The National Road brought thousands of people to Ohio. Travelers often camped out for the night. Others stopped at the many inns along the way. Usually for less than a dollar, they received food and drink, a warm bed, and water for their horses.

You can visit the Columbian House in Waterville. It has welcomed visitors since 1828.
Photo by Roberta Stockwell

Ohio Canals

Canals connected Lake Erie to the Ohio River. They made traveling and shipping faster and easier.

Building Canals

A *canal* is a waterway made by people. It connects natural waterways such as rivers and lakes.

Building canals was very hard work. All the work was done by hand, with shovels. Horses and mules carried off the dirt in wagons. Then the men lined the canal with heavy limestone blocks. If the canal was very long, this took many years. Men came from all over, even other countries, to get jobs on the canals. Workers received thirty cents per day and food for their work. The canal workers lived in shacks or tents along the canal.

Canal Boats

Canal boats were flatboats with a cabin for sleeping and a deck for storing goods and livestock. The boats had no engines. Towpaths were built alongside the canal. The boat was tied to a horse or mule who pulled it along the canal.

The people in Ohio loved their new canals! The boats went at a top speed of four miles an hour. People thought this was very fast. It took about three or four days to make it from Toledo or Cleveland on Lake Erie to a town on the Ohio River.

Canal photo by Kathleen Stockwell

102

A mule on a towpath pulled a boat through the canal.
Photo by John Ivanko

Locks

Locks allowed canal boats to travel up and down hilly country. This is how it worked:

1. The canal boat came into a lock. Gates were closed at both ends.
2. If the boat was going uphill, the water level in the lock was raised. If the boat was going downhill, the water level in the lock was lowered.
3. The water in the lock was made the same level as the next section of the canal.
4. The front gate was opened and the boat traveled onward.

1.   2.   3.   4.

Growing Up Along the Canals

Do you remember the little boy named William in Chapter Five who had the horse named Paddy? He grew up to be a writer. He called his own little boy William. That little boy also grew up to be a famous writer named William Dean Howells.

Howells achieved much fame and fortune in his life. But his happiest days were the ones he spent as a boy growing up along Ohio's canals. He loved the summertime when he and his friends could go swimming in the canal.

Read this quote from his book *A Boy's Town*. When you read it, can you feel the same happiness he once felt?

In the warm summer nights, the water swarmed with laughing, shouting, and screaming boys. . . . They plunged from the bank and splashed in the water . . . some turned somersaults from the decks of the canal boats right into the water. . . . One boy could do a somersault and a half. . . . It was long before the time of electric lighting, . . . but when he touched the water, there came a flash that seemed to light up the universe!

Railroads

Steamboats, canals, and roads helped Ohio grow. But travel was still slower than the people wanted. Even more people wanted to settle in Ohio or travel through it toward the West. Ohio's many farms raised more and more wheat, corn, apples, horses, and cows that had to be sent to market quickly.

Railroads were the solution for faster transportation. Steam-powered engines moved on iron or steel tracks. The train's engine was strong enough to pull many cars loaded with passengers and goods. Trains could go more than ten times faster than canal boats!

The first railroad in Ohio was called the Erie and Kalamazoo Railroad. It connected the city of Toledo to Michigan.

Steam engines moved the trains.

Soon railroads were built between all the major cities in Ohio. "Trunk lines" connected the main railroads to the smaller towns. National railroads connected Ohio to the other states.

The coming of the railroads changed transportation in Ohio forever. Steamboats and canals seemed very slow. Railroad tracks were laid along the Ohio River and Lake Erie. They were also built near the canals.

Soon steamboats disappeared from Ohio's waters. The canals stood silent and empty. Ohio raced faster and faster into the future.

The End of an Era

We should always remember how much steamboats and especially canals changed Ohio. They connected the many growing towns and farms of the state together. They also connected Ohio to the rest of the nation. Whole families with all their possessions traveled down them to new towns. Bushels of farm goods traveled along them to markets in and out of Ohio. They prepared the way for the railroads and superhighways of today.

People cooked, ate, and slept on the trains. They could walk up and down the aisles to help pass the time on a long trip.

New People Come to Ohio

The canals were also important for bringing immigrants from other countries to Ohio. An *immigrant* is a person who moves into a country from another place. The immigrants to Ohio came mostly from Ireland and Germany.

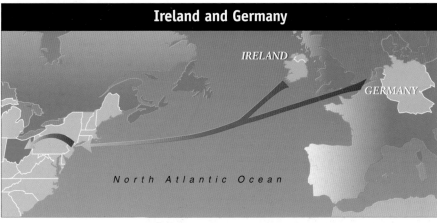

Ireland and Germany

IRELAND

GERMANY

North Atlantic Ocean

The Irish

Ireland was a terrible place to live in during the 1840s. Most of the people there were very poor. Potatoes were their main food. A "blight" hit the potato crop. The potatoes were covered with black spots and rotted in the fields. It was called the Irish Potato Famine. Millions of Irish people starved to death.

The Irish were unhappy for other reasons. Great Britain ruled Ireland. The British treated the Irish very badly. The Irish were not allowed to vote or go to school. They could not practice their Catholic religion.

Millions of Irish men, women, and children boarded ships for the United States. They took the jobs no one else was willing to do. In Ohio, they built the canals and then worked on the canal boats. They also built the railroad tracks and later worked on the trains. They were paid very little.

But the Irish loved Ohio! Many parts of the state had rolling green countryside just like Ireland. They could vote and go to school. They could practice their Catholic faith. Some Irish bought farms. However, most moved to the growing cities. They built businesses, schools, and churches. Many of them went into politics.

Ireland is a small island nation in Europe. People from Ireland are called *Irish*. Use an atlas to find Ireland. What can you learn about the country?

Irish workers get ready to leave for America.
Illustration colored by North Wind Pictures

The Germans Come to Ohio

Germany is a nation in Europe. People from Germany are called *German*.

This Haus-Segen (house blessing) sign can still be found in many German homes today. It is a prayer asking for protection. The two birds at the bottom mean good luck.

An old stone barn reminds us of the German people who came to start a new life in Ohio.

Photo by John Ivanko

Germany was also not a happy place for many people. The nation was divided into small kingdoms. There were many wars. Young men were often drafted into the army to fight these wars. The Germans could not vote or express their opinions about the government. Most of them were too poor to attend school.

Many of the German people were shopkeepers and craftsmen. They settled in Ohio's growing cities. Cincinnati, on the Ohio River, was their favorite town. It reminded them of the many cities that dotted the rivers in their home country.

The German people started many restaurants, meat shops, and bakeries. They also started German-language newspapers and schools. They loved symphony orchestras and the opera. They planted gardens and parks throughout the city. People went there to listen to beautiful music.

Other German immigrants started farms. The Germans were willing to buy land that no one else wanted. They headed for the Black Swamp in northwest Ohio. They cut down the tangle of trees. They dug ditches along the roads to drain water from the swamp. They used steam-powered pumps to drain off even more water.

Once the Black Swamp was drained, the people found that the place had some of the best soil in the state. Soon the area was a patchwork of farms. The people raised wheat, corn, apples, peaches, and livestock. Today, you can travel through much of northwest Ohio and see barns with German names proudly written above the door.

Linking the past and the present

Have you ever gone to a summer concert with your family or friends? Was the concert held in a park or near a river? This custom was brought to Ohio by German immigrants.

Jewish people built places of worship called synagogues. You can still go to Cincinnati and visit the first Jewish synagogue founded in Ohio.

Communal Religions

Many people in Ohio practiced *communal* religions. This meant the people lived, worked, and worshiped together. Every part of their life was tied to their faith. Two of the largest groups were the Shakers and the Amish.

The Shakers

Shaker men and women believed the world would end soon. They did not marry or have children. They lived and worked together as brothers and sisters in one big family. The Shakers shared their possessions. They had prosperous farms and made beautiful furniture.

Shakers loved to sing when they prayed. Their favorite song was "Lord of the Dance." They also loved to dance when they sang. So other people called them "Shakers!" There are no Shakers left in Ohio anymore. But they gave their name to the town of Shaker Heights near Cleveland.

Shaker Heights in 1893 had large wooden buildings, a road, and farmland.

Ohio Portrait

Johnny Appleseed

John Chapman used apple trees to teach others about his faith. He loved God deeply. He could see God everywhere in creation. He loved all people. He was kind to the Indians and the settlers alike. He especially loved animals.

But apple trees were his favorite. He planted apple orchards everywhere he went in Ohio. Sometimes he sold his apple trees for only a few pennies. Other times he gave them away for free. Every tree was a gift of love.

The people of Ohio came to love John Chapman dearly. They even gave him a special name. They called him "Johnny Appleseed."

The Amish

The Amish originally came from Germany and Switzerland. They built neat homes, barns, and fences. They raised animals and farmed. They still live in family farming communities throughout eastern Ohio. Some families sell homemade furniture, food, and crafts.

The Amish do not believe in modern conveniences such as electricity. The women all wear the same style and color of clothing. All the men dress alike, too. They wear homemade clothes with hooks instead of buttons and zippers. Many families teach their children at home. The Amish use black buggies pulled by horses instead of cars and trucks.

Girls gather on a porch.

Amish families walk to church.

Switzerland is a country high in the Alps. The Alps are high mountains in Europe.

No Place for Ohio's Indians

Many people had found a home in the Gateway State of Ohio. But one group of people was no longer welcome. The Ohio Indians were told to leave their homeland forever.

Some Americans did not like the Indians. They thought they might start another war. Others wanted all their land. So Congress passed a law called the Indian Removal Act. President Andrew Jackson signed the bill into law. The Indians had to sell their land and move west across the Mississippi River.

Most of the Miami, Delaware, and Mingo had already left the state. But the Ottawa and Wyandot still lived in their old villages. Many Shawnee had settled down on farms. These tribes did not want to leave. They wanted to stay in Ohio, but no one would listen to them.

The tribes were all forced to move to the Kansas Territory. Many people died along the way. Some did not live through the first cold winter in Kansas. But the men and women who survived built farms and ranches. They kept their ancient customs alive.

112

People now know that the Indian removal from Ohio was a terrible thing. Can you think of anything that could have been done to prevent this from happening?

Activity

Writing about Childhood Memories

William Dean Howells fondly remembered his Ohio childhood. Imagine that you are all grown up. Write your own story about growing up as a child in modern Ohio. Remember that canals made William Dean Howells very happy. Be sure to include the things that make you the happiest about growing up in Ohio.

Chapter 6 Review

1. Why was Ohio called the Gateway State?
2. People invented ways to travel faster and better. This was called the _____ _____.
3. What are the four main types of boats the people used?
4. What was the name of the first road built in Ohio?
5. What was the name of the long road that went from Maryland all the way to Vandalia, Illinois?
6. A waterway dug by people is called a _____.
7. What allowed canal boats to travel up and down hilly country?
8. After the railroads came, what was the fastest way to travel in early Ohio?
9. What contributions did the Irish and Germans make to Ohio?
10. What is another name for a grade school?
11. Schools run by a church are called _____ schools.
12. What early book taught children to read and how to act?
13. What two early communal religious groups lived in Ohio? Do they still live here today?
14. What was the Indian Removal Act? How did it affect the Ohio Indian people?

Geography Tie-In

On the map on page 102, see where the two major canals ran. Then compare that map with a modern road map of Ohio. Do you live near one of the old canal routes? What major cities are on these same routes? What roads would you take to get to them today?

Chapter 7

THE TIME
1840–1865

PEOPLE TO KNOW

President William Henry
   Harrison
John Tyler
Benjamin Lundy
Harriet Beecher Stowe
President Abraham
   Lincoln
Mother Bickerdyke
Clement Vallandingham
Captain John Morgan
Fighting McCooks
Johnny Clem
Ulysses S. Grant
W. Tecumseh Sherman
John Wilkes Booth

PLACES TO LOCATE

North Bend
Bolivia
Troy
Piqua
Sidney
Xenia
Northern States
Southern States
Charleston
Fort Sumter
Shiloh
Georgia
North Carolina

Timeline of Events

1840
William Henry Harrison
is elected president of
the U.S.

1840

1845

1841
Harrison dies after only
forty days in office.

1850
Fugitive Slave Act passed
Underground Railroad is in use

114

Chapter 7

Ohio in the Civil War

WORDS TO UNDERSTAND
inaugurate
free state
slave state
slave
plantation
prejudice
abolitionist
sympathy
bestseller
assassinated

1852
Harriet Beecher Stowe's *Uncle Tom's Cabin* is published.

1860
Abraham Lincoln is elected president of the U.S.

1861
Fort Sumter is attacked.

1862
Battle of Shiloh
(Tennessee)

1864
Sherman's "March to the Sea"

1865
Lincoln is assassinated.

1855

1860

1865

1863
Vallandingham runs for governor of Ohio and is defeated.

1861–1865
Civil War

The Log Cabin Campaign

The year 1840 was a happy one for many Ohioans. It was the first time that a man from Ohio ran for president of the United States. The man was William Henry Harrison. Because he had fought Tecumseh's confederation at Tippecanoe, Indiana, they gave him the nickname of "Tippecanoe."

After the War of 1812, Harrison had settled on a farm in North Bend overlooking the Ohio River. There he and his wife raised their ten children.

Harrison also worked in politics. He served in the Ohio legislature and the United States Senate. He was even the ambassador to Bolivia, a country in South America. He brought a bright blue macaw home with him from the jungle. The bird flew in the trees near the Harrison family farmhouse.

Some people outside of Ohio made fun of Harrison when he ran for the presidency. They thought people from Ohio were still pioneers. They told him to stay home in his log cabin and drink homemade cider.

Harrison's supporters decided to use the insults in their campaign to help Harrison win the election. They built log cabins as floats. They carried these floats in campaign rallies. The whole campaign became known as the "Log Cabin Campaign."

Harrison was a member of the Whig Party. His vice president was a man named John Tyler. So people shouted, "Tippecanoe and Tyler Too!" as their campaign slogan. Tens of thousands of people came to see old General Harrison at rallies throughout the state. They cheered and remembered him for his victories over Tecumseh and the British.

William Henry Harrison served as president of the United States for only forty days.

Illustration colored by North Wind Pictures

Harrison Wins the Election

Harrison was elected president. But he died only forty days after he was *inaugurated,* or sworn into office. Americans were very sad. This was the first time a president had died in office. Harrison was buried near his home in North Bend.

The people of Ohio would soon stop looking back to their pioneer past. They had to look to the future and face the growing problem of slavery.

The Problem of Slavery

The United States had *free states* and *slave states*. The people in the free states in the North did not have *slaves*. In the slave states in the South, there were many slaves. Whole families were slaves. Grandmothers and grandfathers, mothers and fathers, children and their cousins—they worked all of their lives. They had no freedom at all.

The ancestors of the slaves had been brought from Africa to work on *plantations*. The slaves did much work for the people who owned them. They worked in the fields. They cooked, cleaned, and sewed in the plantation houses. The women took care of the slave owner's children. The men often worked as carpenters, blacksmiths, and shipbuilders.

A slave is a person held in bondage for life. Slaves were bought and sold. They were the property of their owner.

A plantation was a farm in the South. Some plantations were very large, but most were average-sized farms. Plantations grew crops like cotton, tobacco, sugar, and rice.

African Americans in Ohio

The Northwest Ordinance had banned slavery from Ohio. But many people were still *prejudiced* against African Americans. They passed laws that made life difficult for them. African Americans could not sue in a court or serve on a jury. The children usually could not attend the state's public schools.

Even with such prejudice, many African Americans came to Ohio anyway. Some of them had been freed by their owners. Others were runaways who had escaped from their masters.

Freed slaves started towns and farms in Troy, Piqua, Sidney, and Xenia. They worked as cooks in inns along the National Road. They loaded goods on and off steamboats on the Ohio River. They guided horses along the canals. A runaway slave named John Malvin even became the captain of his own canal boat in Cleveland.

Life was not easy for these hardworking people. But they would rather be free in Ohio than slaves in the South.

Slaves picked cotton in the South.
Illustration colored by North Wind Pictures

The Underground Railroad

Slaves in the South knew that crossing north across the Ohio River meant freedom. Many slaves ran away to Ohio. Others journeyed north through Ohio and went on to Canada. Slavery was against the law in Canada

The slaves called this dangerous path to freedom the Underground Railroad. They imagined that they were on a train taking them northward. The river banks and canal towpaths they walked along were the "train tracks."

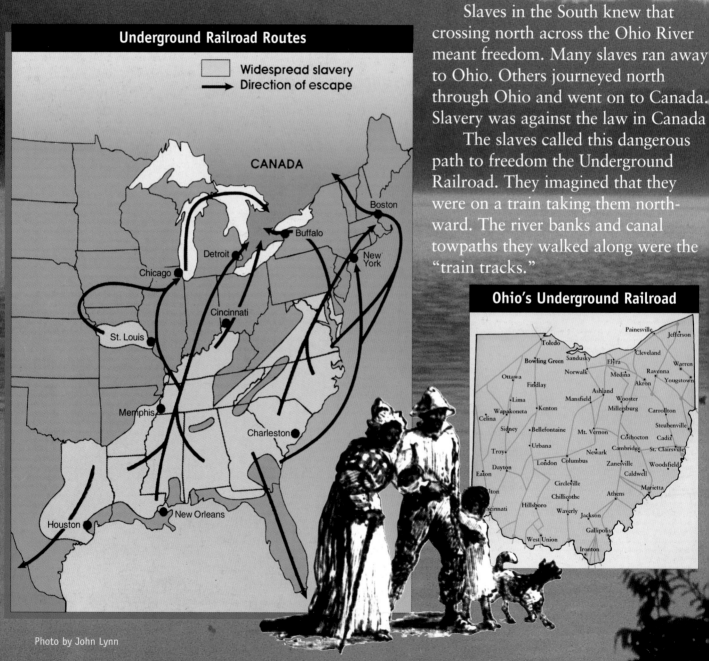

Underground Railroad Routes

☐ Widespread slavery
→ Direction of escape

CANADA

Boston
Buffalo
Detroit
New York
Chicago
Cincinnati
St. Louis
Memphis
Charleston
New Orleans
Houston

Ohio's Underground Railroad

Painesville
Jefferson
Toledo
Cleveland
Bowling Green Sandusky Elyra Warren
Ottawa Norwalk Medina Ravenna Youngstown
Findlay Akron
Lima Ashland
Wapakoneta Kenton Mansfield Wooster
Celina Millersburg Carrollton
Sidney Bellefontaine Mt. Vernon Coshocton Steubenville
Urbana Cadiz
Troy Newark Cambridge St. Clairsville
Dayton London Columbus Zanesville Woodsfield
Eaton Caldwell
Circleville Marietta
lton Chillicothe Athens
ncinnati Hillsboro Waverly Jackson
West Union Gallipolis
Ironton

Photo by John Lynn

118

wheat, beef, cheese, and apples. Ohio also had factories that turned out even more products that soldiers needed. Look at the map of Ohio and see how many things you can name that were used in the war effort.

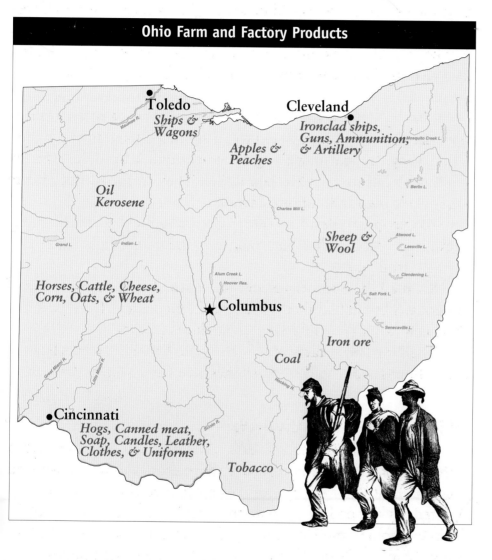

Ohio Farm and Factory Products

Toledo
Ships & Wagons

Cleveland
Ironclad ships, Guns, Ammunition, & Artillery

Apples & Peaches

Oil Kerosene

Sheep & Wool

Horses, Cattle, Cheese, Corn, Oats, & Wheat

★ Columbus

Iron ore

Coal

Cincinnati
Hogs, Canned meat, Soap, Candles, Leather, Clothes, & Uniforms

Tobacco

Copperheads

Not everyone in Ohio supported the Union. Some young men in the southern part of the state joined the Confederate army. Other people who stayed behind thought the North should let the South go without a fight. These people were called "Copperheads." A copperhead is a poisonous snake that strikes

Mary Ann Bickerdyke

In church one Sunday, Mary Ann Bickerdyke heard about the awful conditions in army hospitals. Church members collected bandages and medicine. A week later, she was on a train headed to an army camp.

What she saw at the camp made her angry. Wounded men, covered with flies, slept on dirty straw on the ground. Mrs. Bickerdyke and some soldiers sawed barrels in half and filled them with water. They washed the men and made clean beds in the tents.

Mary Ann organized more hospital camps in other places. Once she led eleven steamboats loaded with doctors, nurses, and medical supplies. For four years she took care of Union soldiers. She made hot soup, bread, and pies. Up and down the Mississippi and Ohio Rivers, homesick soldiers began calling her "Mother."

The Nasby Letters

David Ross Locke was a young newspaperman. He worked for a paper called *The Jeffersonian* in Findlay. He wrote a famous column called "The Nasby Letters." He pretended to be a Copperhead named "Reverend Petroleum Vesuvius Nasby." "Petroleum" means slippery oil, and "Vesuvius" is the name of an ancient volcano. Can you see why he called himself that silly name?

Reverend Nasby said such funny things that soon most people were laughing at the Copperheads. President Lincoln loved the letters so much that he memorized them by heart.

without warning. Why do you suppose these people were called Copperheads?

Clement Vallandingham was a United States congressman from Dayton. He was the leader of the Copperheads. He thought the Civil War was wrong. He worried that the war would make the president and the government too strong. He traveled throughout Ohio speaking against the war.

Union soldiers arrested Vallandingham. They sent him south to join the Confederate army. Vallandingham escaped and made his way back to Ohio. He was very angry at President Lincoln. He ran for governor of Ohio. He promised to take Ohio out of the war if he became governor. Luckily for the Union, Vallandingham lost the election.

President Lincoln was very happy when he heard the news. He said, "Glory to God in the highest! Ohio has saved the Union!"

Morgan's Raid

Ohio gave men and equipment to fight the war. Happily, no major battles were fought in the state. But Ohio was invaded by Confederate raiders in the summer of 1863.

Morgan's Raiders rode into Washington County and looted homes and businesses.

Captain John Morgan led 2,500 men. For two weeks, they raced on horseback from one end of the state to the other.

They were in desperate need of supplies. They stole food, coffee, sugar, clothing, tobacco, and horses. They also took things they could never really use. Here is one account of some of the strange things Morgan's men stole:

> *One man carried a bird-cage with three canaries in it . . . another slung seven pairs of skates around his neck and laughed about his prizes!*

Union soldiers finally captured Morgan and most of his raiders. He was sent to a prison in Columbus. But the daring captain and six of his men dug a tunnel out of the prison and escaped back to Kentucky.

The Fighting McCooks

The McCook family was a large one. Daniel McCook had ten sons. His brother John McCook had seven sons. They all lived close to one another. People called them the "Tribe of Dan" and the "Tribe of John."

When the Civil War broke out, all of the McCooks went off to join the Union army. Three became generals. Sadly, Daniel McCook was killed while trying to capture Morgan's Raiders. You can visit the McCook Family Museum to learn more about this brave fighting clan.

The Drummer Boy of Shiloh

Johnny Clem of Newark was only nine years old when the Civil War started. He made a drum out of an old keg and whittled a pair of drumsticks. He ran away from home and drummed for the Union army as they marched into battle.

On Easter Sunday morning at the Battle of Shiloh, a shell burst and shattered Johnny's drum. The soldiers gave him a new drum and called him "Johnny Shiloh." When the war ended, Johnny came back to Newark. He went back to school wearing the medal given to him by the army.

Leaders in the War

Ohio sent many politicians to Washington to help in the war effort. President Lincoln chose Salmon P. Chase as the secretary of the treasury. He decided how to pay for the war. Edwin M. Stanton was the secretary of war. He laid out the war strategy.

Even more important for the Union, Lincoln found his two best generals in the state of Ohio. Ulysses S. Grant and William Tecumseh Sherman led the Union army in its greatest victories against the Confederate army.

General Ulysses S. Grant

Ulysses S. Grant was the toughest general ever seen in the Union army. He liked to smoke cigars and drink whiskey. Some people did not like Grant. They told Lincoln to fire him. But Lincoln said he wished all his generals fought like Grant. The Ohio general was fearless! His determination led the Union to victory.

Despite his many victories in battle, Grant remained an Ohio farm boy at heart. In fact, he never wanted to be a soldier. That was something his father had forced him to do. He sent his son off to West Point when the boy was only seventeen. Grant would have preferred staying home, plowing the

General Ulysses S. Grant stands outside a tent.

Ohio Portrait

William Tecumseh Sherman

Sherman was born in Lancaster, Ohio in 1820. He was one of thirteen children. His father named him Tecumseh after the great Indian chief. Cump was a nickname for Tecumseh. Cump's father hoped his son would one day be a great man like Tecumseh.

Sadly, Cump's father died when he was just a little boy. The child was sent to live with a family called the Ewings. His adopted parents decided that little Cump needed a more respectable name. They called him William.

William grew up to be one of the greatest Union generals in the Civil War. He directed the famous March to the Sea. He sent his soldiers through Georgia, destroying everything in their path. This march finally broke the spirit of the South.

In 1865, Sherman accepted the surrender of the Confederate army in North Carolina. Like his namesake, General William Tecumseh Sherman had truly become a great man.

fields and raising horses. His happiest memories were of his childhood on his father's farm outside of Georgetown. Here is how he described his early life:

> When I was seven or eight years of age, I began hauling all the wood used in the house and shops . . . When about eleven years old, I was strong enough to hold a plough. From that age on, I did all the work done with horses, such as breaking up the land, ploughing corn and potatoes, bringing in the crops when harvested, hauling the wood, and sawing wood for stoves . . . while still attending school.

Grant remembered how important a horse is to a farmer. When Confederate General Robert E. Lee surrendered to Grant in Virginia in the spring of 1865, Grant let all the Confederate soldiers keep their horses. He knew they would need them to plow the fields when they got back home.

The Confederate army surrendered first to Grant in Virginia, and then to Sherman in North Carolina.

General Grant let Confederate soldiers keep their horses.

The Civil War Comes to an End

In April, 1865, the Civil War finally came to an end. The Confederacy was defeated. The Union was victorious. Slavery was outlawed. All the slaves were freed and made American citizens.

More than 35,000 young men from Ohio had died fighting to save the Union. The people of the state had raised more than ten million dollars to help pay for the war. Food and manufactured goods from Ohio had fed, clothed, and armed the Union soldiers. Now the long and terrible war that had divided the nation was over. The people of Ohio celebrated with parades and speeches in every town.

But joy quickly turned to sorrow. President Lincoln was *assassinated* only days after the war ended. A man named John Wilkes Booth shot Lincoln while he was watching a play at Ford's Theater in Washington, D.C.

After the funeral, Lincoln's body was taken by train to his hometown of Springfield, Illinois. The black-draped coffin passed through many towns in Ohio. Thousands and thousands

President Lincoln was shot while sitting with his wife Mary in a private theater booth. The Civil War had just ended. The man who shot Lincoln jumped down to the stage and broke his leg. He went out a back door and rode away on a horse.

of people waited to see the train in Cleveland. Others lined up for over six hours to see the coffin laid out at the state capital in Columbus. Many more waited along the train tracks. They waved goodbye to their beloved leader as he sped past them toward his final resting place.

The people of Ohio wondered, "What will become of the nation after the Civil War?" Although no one could be certain of the future, they knew that Ohio would play a leading role in the nation—just as the state had played a leading role during the Civil War.

What do you think?

Slavery was a terrible problem for the United States. Why do you think people were once allowed to own slaves?

$200 Reward.

RANAWAY from the subscriber, on the night of Thursday, the 30th of Sepember,

FIVE NEGRO SLAVES,

To-wit: one Negro man, his wife, and three children

The man is a black negro, full height, very erect, his face a little thin. He is about forty years of age, and calls himself *Washington Reed*, and is known by the name of Washington. He is probably well dressed, possibly takes with him an ivory headed cane, and is of good address. Several of his teeth are gone.

Mary, his wife, is about thirty years of age, a bright mulatto woman, and quite stout and strong.

The oldest of the children is a boy, of the name of FIELDING, twelve years of age, a dark mulatto, with heavy eyelids. He probably wore a new cloth cap.

MATILDA, the second child, is a girl, six years of age, rather a dark mulatto, but a bright and smart looking child.

MALCOLM, the youngest, is a boy, four years old, a lighter mulatto than the last, and about equally as bright. He probably also wore a cloth cap. If examined, he will be found to have a swelling at the navel.

Washington and Mary have lived at or near St. Louis, with the subscriber, for about 15 years.

It is supposed that they are making their way to Chicago, and that a white man accompanies them, that they will travel chiefly at night, and most probably in a covered wagon.

A reward of $150 will be paid for their apprehension, so that I can get them, if taken within one hundred miles of St. Louis, and $200 if taken beyond that, and secured so that I can get them, and other reasonable additional charges, if delivered to the subscriber, or to THOMAS ALLEN, Esq., at St. Louis, Mo. The above negroes, for the last few years, have been in possession of Thomas Allen, Esq., of St. Louis.

WM. RUSSELL.

ST. LOUIS, Oct. 1, 1847.

Activity

Singing Along with History

Before radio, television, and movies were invented, people entertained themselves by getting together to sing songs. Many songs were about politics. They sang them at political rallies for their candidates. The slaves sang songs, too. Some of these songs talked about the Underground Railroad.

Your library might have songbooks that have these old songs. Make it a class project to see how many songs you can find and how many you can learn to sing yourselves!

Chapter 7 Review

1. What was the Log Cabin Campaign?
2. Was Ohio a slave state or a free state?
3. Why was slavery a problem for the United States?
4. What was the Underground Railroad?
5. What did the book *Uncle Tom's Cabin* have to do with the Civil War?
6. Who was president of the United States during the Civil War?
7. What contributions did Ohio make to the Union during the Civil War?
8. Who were the Copperheads?
9. Name two famous Union generals from Ohio.
10. What terrible event occurred just a few days after the Civil War ended?

Geography Tie-In

Look at the map of where the main Underground Railroad paths ran in Ohio. Then compare it to a modern road map of Ohio. Do you live near one of the Underground Railroad paths? If you do, check to see if there are any historical markers in your area that point to a stop on the Underground Railroad.

Industry and Immigrants

Chapter 8

THE TIME
1865–1915

PEOPLE TO KNOW
Ulysses S. Grant
Rutherford B. Hayes
"Lemonade Lucy" Hayes
James A. Garfield
Benjamin Harrison
William McKinley
Catherine Scott Harrison
John D. Rockefeller
Paul Laurence Dunbar
Annie Oakley
Victoria Woodhull

PLACES TO LOCATE
Appalachia
Fremont
Spiegel Grove
Mentor
Canton
Cincinnati
Cleveland
Toledo
Columbus
Dayton
Akron
Ireland
Germany
Poland
Czech Republic
Hungary
Russia
Italy
Greece
Albania

Timeline of Events

1868
Grant is elected president.

1873
Ohio State University is founded.

1876
Hayes is elected president.

1880
Garfield is elected president.

1865   1870   1875   1880

1870
Goodrich Rubber Co. opens.

1872
Victoria Woodhull runs for president. Grant is re-elected.

1874
Women's Christian Temperance Union is founded.

Chapter 8

WORDS TO UNDERSTAND
politics
industry
tariff
import
agriculture
veterinary
tenement
stockbroker

Children long ago liked to blow bubbles just like you do.

1888
Harrison is elected president.

1898
Spanish American War

1900
McKinley is re-elected president.

1890   1895   1900   1905   1915

1881
Garfield is assassinated.

1896
McKinley is elected president.

1901
McKinley is assassinated.

131

Ohio Leads the Nation

After the Civil War, Ohio still had many farms, but factories were becoming more important every day. People from near and far wanted to move to Ohio. They knew it was a good place for industry and a good place to find work. They also believed that Ohio would lead the nation in *politics*. Politics has to do with government.

Ohio had many qualities that made it a leader in *industry*. You probably already know that industry has to do with work, especially work in factories, mines, and transportation.

Let's see why so many people thought politics and industry were so important after the Civil War.

The Heart of It All

• **Civil War Heritage**—Ohio had contributed so much to save the Union. The best Union generals had come from Ohio. Food, money, and factory goods poured out of the state to help the North win. Now everyone expected Ohio to continue to help America grow.

• **Location**—Look at Ohio's location on a map of the United States. Ohio is truly the Gateway State. People and goods move east and west through Ohio. They also move north and south through the state. Do you see how Lake Erie and the Ohio River connect Ohio to the world? That's why people to this day call Ohio the "Heart of It All!"

Burning coal made it possible to run factories in Ohio.

•**Natural Resources**—Do you remember what you learned about our natural resources in Chapter One? Geologists believe that it took millions of years to build up natural resources under Ohio's soil. Coal, natural gas, oil, and so many other resources lay under the ground. Everything Ohio needed for modern industry was right here.

•**Transportation**—Ohio's hard work in building roads, canals, and trains now paid off. People who wanted to build factories and sell their products to the world came to Ohio. Good roads and shipping lines were everywhere. Trucks, trains, and boats loaded with products were sent from ports in Cincinnati, Cleveland, and Toledo.

•**People**—Ohioans were a hardworking people. They had been farmers, canal builders, and railroad workers since pioneer days. Now they were ready to live in big cities and work in industry. Many more immigrants wanted to come to Ohio and help build up the state even more.

Ohio, the Mother of Presidents

If you asked most Americans who they would want as president after the Civil War, they probably would have said; "A man from Ohio!" Five men from Ohio were elected president between 1865 (the year the war ended) and 1900. They all had the following traits:

⚙ **Union Soldiers**—Each man had been a Union soldier in the Civil War. The American people thought this meant the men were loyal Americans.

⚙ **Republicans**—They were all members of the Republican Party. This was Abraham Lincoln's party.

⚙ **Pro-business**—The presidents passed laws to help business grow. They wanted low taxes on business and the wealthy.

But, they favored high *tariffs* on *imports*. A tariff is a tax placed on imported goods. Imported goods are products brought to America from another country. Tariffs can make imported goods more expensive to buy than American ones. This helps Americans sell more of their own goods.

Ulysses S. Grant

When President Grant was born, his parents named him Hiram Ulysses Grant. He did not like his initials—H.U.G. When he went to college, the school incorrectly wrote Ulysses Simpson Grant on one of his forms. He used that name for the rest of his life.

Grant did not want to be president any more than he wanted to be a soldier. But the American people wanted him to be their leader. They thought he could help make the nation strong after the Civil War. Union veterans especially loved him. They sang this popular campaign song:

So boys a final bumper
While we all in chorus chant,
For our next president we nominate
Our Own Ulysses Grant.

President Ulysses S. Grant and his family pose for a painting.

One day President Grant was speeding his horse and buggy down a Washington, D.C. street. A policeman stopped to give him a ticket. When the officer realized that it was the president, he apologized. But President Grant told the policeman he was doing his job and insisted on taking the ticket.

Grant was a good general, but he was not a good president. Some of the people he hired to work for him were dishonest. They stole money from the American government. Grant left office a sad man.

President Grant was born in this home in Point Pleasant.

Rutherford B. Hayes

When Hayes ran for president, people had not forgotten the Civil War. Union soldiers were still stationed in the South. Hayes promised that he would remove the last soldiers from the South if he was elected.

The Hayes family liked to have many people visit the White House, but sometimes it got so hectic that President Hayes locked himself in the bathroom so he could get his work done!

Hayes was happy to return to his beautiful home in Fremont when his term was over. You can still visit Spiegel Grove, his twenty-five acre farm, with its forests, fields, and ponds.

President Rutherford Hayes

Lucy Webb Hayes

Lucy was married to President Rutherford Hayes. They had five children. Lucy wanted to make the White House a beautiful home for her own family. She also wanted to make it a home for the entire nation. She held many dinners and parties there.

Mrs. Hayes never served alcohol of any kind at her White House parties. People called her "Lemonade Lucy." She was such a wonderful entertainer that people called her the "First Lady." This has been the name of the president's wife ever since.

Mrs. Lucy Webb Hayes

James A. Garfield

Young James Garfield knew much hardship as a child. His father died when he was only a boy, and he was raised by his mother. He loved his mother very much, and later brought her to live in the White House with him.

Garfield had little time for grade school. He had to work on his family's farm. All by himself, he cleared the land and planted crops.

Garfield finally made enough money to go to college and become a lawyer. He bought a farm in Mentor for his wife and children. Garfield is famous for writing with both hands at once. He could write Greek with one hand and Latin with the other!

People liked this broad-shouldered man. They called him a farmer and a scholar. They elected him president, hoping he would make America better. Sadly, Garfield was shot by a man in a train station. He died less than a year after taking office.

President James A. Garfield

Benjamin Harrison

Little Ben Harrison grew up on a farm right next to the home of his grandfather, William Henry Harrison. Do you remember that William Harrison had been president of the United States for a short time? One of Ben's earliest memories was riding in a wagon with his grandpa as he ran for president.

President Harrison and his wife, Caroline, modernized the White House. When they moved in, it was crawling with insects and even rats. They had to hire a professional rat catcher! They had electricity put in the White House. Stories say that they were afraid of the electricity and asked servants to turn the light switches on and off.

Harrison remembered all his life how important it was for a politician to meet the people. As president, he traveled for thousands of miles meeting Americans. He especially liked going to the Southern States. He tried hard to heal the wounds left by the Civil War.

President Benjamin Harrison

Photo by Art Weber

William McKinley

William McKinley loved cigars, but he never had his picture taken with one. He thought it would set a bad example.

McKinley did not like campaigning. When he ran for president, he stayed home in Canton. His house had a wide front porch. He went out there to talk with visitors and reporters. So people called it the "Front Porch Campaign."

Americans grew to love their quiet president. He led them in the Spanish-American War. He sent troops to Cuba to free that country from Spanish control. Sadly, McKinley was shot and killed while visiting Buffalo, New York.

President William McKinley

Ohio's State Flower

Did you ever wonder why the red carnation is Ohio's state flower? The answer is simple. It was William McKinley's favorite flower. He wore one every day. He loved its bright color and spicy fragrance. He also thought it brought him good luck.

There was only one day that McKinley was not wearing a carnation. It was the day he was killed. He had taken it off to give to a little girl. After his death, the people of Ohio wanted to pay a special tribute to their fallen leader. They made the scarlet carnation their state flower.

Industry Booms

Ohio's presidents all tried to help industry grow. Factories in Ohio produced goods that could be sold all over the United States. Each major city in Ohio used the natural resources, transportation network, and people in the area to set up important industries.

Cincinnati—Ohio's Largest City

Cincinnati began as an army post called Fort Washington. By the Civil War, it was known as the "Queen City" on the Ohio River. Steamboats lined up for more than a mile along its docks. The ships brought immigrants to Ohio and took farm goods to market.

The city continued to grow during the Civil War. Union soldiers poured south through Cincinnati. Factories in the town turned out uniforms, guns, wagons, food, and cannons for the troops.

After the war, more and more people moved to Cincinnati. Local factories made clothes, soap, and musical instruments.

With so many farms nearby, Cincinnati also became a center for packing meat and canning foods. People who lived in big cities could buy their food from a grocery store.

Cincinnati was a great success. But it was also very crowded. More than 300,000 people lived there. It soon became known as the most crowded city in America.

Cincinnati was once the most crowded city in America.
Illustration colored by North Wind Pictures

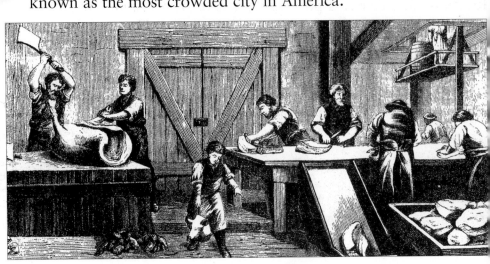

There were many pork-packing plants in Cincinnati. The city was called "Porkopolis" for many years. What would the place smell like? What would it be like to work there?

Cleveland—Ohio's Second Largest City

Cleveland was founded in 1796 by people from New England. It was at the mouth of the beautiful Cuyahoga River. The town grew slowly until canals were built throughout Ohio. Cleveland then became a gateway for people and goods moving through the state.

During the Civil War, the people of Cleveland worked hard to make guns and cannons for the Union soldiers. After the war, the city became known for making steel and building ships. Oil refining also became a top industry.

Like Cincinnati, Cleveland became successful, but at a price. The beautiful town that once stood around a village green now had crowded streets and slums. The steel mills and oil refineries filled the air with black smoke. The people of Cleveland would have to work hard to clean up their town.

What clues can you see in this picture about the way people in Cleveland made a living? Do you see boats that carried goods in and out of the city? Do you see factories where the goods were produced?

Illustration colored by North Wind Pictures

Toledo—Ohio's Third Largest City

Toledo had begun as a trading post at the mouth of the Maumee River. Stores were set up along the river to trade with the local Ottawa, Miami, and Wyandot Indians. All the trading posts were joined into the city of Toledo in 1833.

The people soon built industries around the town's great location. Toledo was a port on Lake Erie. The Miami and Erie Canal also started there. A dozen major railroad lines met in Toledo. The people of the city specialized in industries related to transportation. Wagons, ships, and eventually automobiles became the top goods produced in Toledo's many factories.

Toledo also stood in the middle of rich farm land. Grain elevators quickly rose along the river-front. Toledo also stood on sandy soil. Sand is one of the key elements in making glass. By 1900, Toledo was known as the "Glass Capital of the World."

Wagons were made in Toledo and shipped to many other cities.

Ohio State University

Columbus became known as the home of the Ohio State University. President Lincoln had passed a law that gave states land out west. The states could sell the land and then use the money to build an **agricultural** college. Students could learn the best ways to raise and sell crops and animals to provide food for people.

Today, students study agriculture, medicine, and many other subjects at the university. The school has one of the finest **veterinary** hospitals in the world.

"Hello, I am Natty."
A few years ago, Natty became very sick. His owner took him to the veterinary hospital at Ohio State University. The doctors operated on the little dog and soon he was well again.

Although Toledo was only half the size of Cincinnati, it had all the same problems of a much bigger town. The streets were unpaved. There were few policemen or firemen. The people of Toledo would work hard to improve their town in the next century.

A circus came to Toledo in 1900. Everyone dressed up to watch the elephants parade through the streets.

Columbus—the Fourth Largest City

Before the Civil War, Columbus was important for two reasons. It was the state capital. It was also a main stop on the National Road. Hotels and stables lined the streets.

Columbus grew quickly during the Civil War. Thousands of young men came into the city to enlist in the Union army. Businesses were started to feed and supply the soldiers.

The boom continued after the war. The city's central location and its many railroads made it a great place to start factories. Train cars filled with coal and oil came into Columbus from the nearby hill country. Canned food, metal products, and mining equipment became top industries. Later, Columbus made airplane and car parts.

Like Ohio's other big cities, Columbus had problems. Workers were paid very little. They were crowded into dingy apartment buildings near the railroads and factories. The worst slums were along the muddy banks of the Scioto River. The river ran right through the center of town. By 1900, the people of Columbus were looking for ways to make their city beautiful once again.

Tenement life was hard, but a friend made things a lot easier.

Big cities had many slum areas. Workers lived in crowded apartment buildings called **tenements**. There was no air conditioning. Upstairs apartments got very hot, so people often slept up on the roof in the cool night air.

Dayton and Akron

Two more Ohio towns were beginning to boom by 1900. Dayton began as a small farming and trade center along the Miami River. But one invention changed the little town into a great city. The invention was the cash register. John Patterson opened the National Cash Register Company. Soon Dayton was making and selling cash registers to almost every country in the world.

Akron was also becoming a big factory town. People from New England founded Akron. The town was mainly a place where farmers came to have their flour milled. That all changed in 1870 when Benjamin Franklin Goodrich stood and watched his neighbor's house burn to

Cash registers added up the cost of what people bought at a store.

the ground. He decided right then and there to start a rubber hose factory in Akron. The hoses were needed to carry water to the fire. The city soon became the "Rubber Capital of the World."

New Immigrants Flock to Ohio

Many people heard about the growing towns and booming industries in Ohio. They wanted to live and work in Ohio. Once again the state became a gateway to immigrants from near and far who wanted a better life for themselves and their families.

People Come from the Farms

Some people came into the cities from nearby farms. Many young men and women were tired of the hard work on their parents' farms. They wanted to make more money in the big city. Some wanted to go to school and start their own businesses. Others were certain that life in a large town had to be more exciting than life on the farm. They wanted to meet new people and go to new places.

Many people moved from the farms into town. What kinds of transportation do you see in this picture?

People Come from the South

Many former slaves and their families moved into Ohio at this time. Life in the South was very hard for them after the Civil War. Land was expensive and difficult to buy. Many African Americans came to Ohio's growing cities. They hoped to find work in the booming factories or on the railroads.

African American children and their parents moved to Ohio from the South. Life was still very hard.

This black man is part of a crew of men who built roads in the 1880s.

Ohio Portrait

Paul Laurence Dunbar

Paul Laurence Dunbar was the child of former slaves. He spent most of his life in Dayton. More than anything else, he wanted to be a great writer. But many Ohioans were very prejudiced against black people. He could not find a job as a writer. Instead, he spent most of his life working as an elevator operator. In his spare time, Paul wrote beautiful poems about Ohio's changing seasons. He also wrote love poems.

In his most famous poem, some people think he was talking about himself. Others say he was describing how hard it is to live with prejudice. What do you think he means?

Sympathy

I know why the caged bird sings, ah me,
When his wing is bruised and his bosom sore,
When he beats his bars and he would be free;
It is not a carol of joy or glee,
But a prayer that he sends from his heart's deep core,
But a plea, that upward to Heaven he flings
I know why the caged bird sings.

143

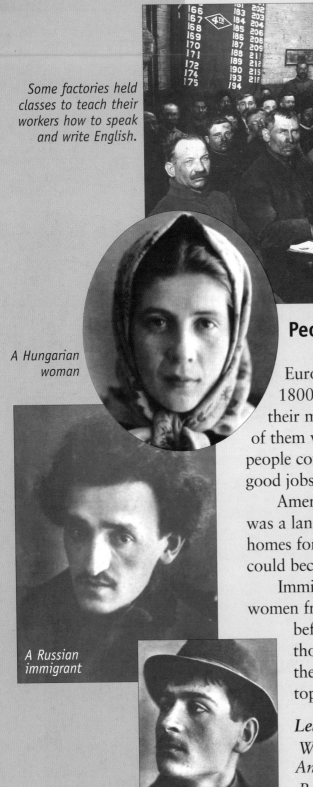

Some factories held classes to teach their workers how to speak and write English.

A Hungarian woman

A Russian immigrant

An Albanian farmer

People Come from Europe and Beyond

After the Civil War, most immigrants came from Europe. Europe was not a happy place to be in the late 1800s. The common people could not vote or even speak their minds about politics. There were few schools, and most of them were open only to the very wealthy. In some places, people could not practice their own religion. There were few good jobs, and many people were very poor.

America became a dream for millions of Europeans. Here was a land where everyone could find work. They could buy homes for their families. Their children could go to school. They could become American citizens and vote in every election.

Immigrants from Europe poured into Ohio. Young men and women from Ireland and Germany came just as they had done before the Civil War. But now they were joined by thousands of people from other European countries and the Middle East. Their hard work made Ohio one of the top industrial states in the nation.

Leaving Poland for America

When I was six, my family left Poland to set sail for America to join my papa.

Before we left mama brought me and my two older brothers, Tomek and Josef, together by the fire. She lit two candles and sang a song to the angels. It was

Mayor Tom Johnson of Cleveland

Tom Johnson's life was a lot like Samuel Jones's life. He wanted to go to school but had to drop out after the third grade. He was a poor boy who had to help support his family. He got his first job working on a *streetcar*.

Young Tom Johnson wanted to be a success. He knew he could make a great deal of money if only he could invent something that would help make people's lives easier.

Tom didn't have to look far for his new invention. He created a glass fare box for streetcars. People could climb onto the streetcar and drop their fare right in the box. The driver saw the fare through the glass. He did not have to stop and take the fare from people. Soon Johnson was a millionaire.

Tom Johnson could have retired and spent the rest of his life enjoying his wealth. But he wanted to help people. He moved to Cleveland and ran for mayor as a Democrat. He promised he would pass laws to improve the city. He was elected to the first of four terms as mayor. He:

A streetcar was a horse-drawn or electric vehicle that ran on tracks in a city. It was the main way workers traveled in towns before automobiles.

- Built public parks along the waterfront.
- Paved the streets.
- Put in the first electric streetlights of any American city.
- Started citywide garbage pickup.

Mayor Johnson started a garbage collection service. It kept city streets cleaner.

Young boys in Cleveland saw many changes to their town after Mayor Johnson was elected.

Another man from Ohio was running for president. Big "Will" Taft was a likeable man. He loved to study history and law. He dreamed of one day becoming a great judge. He also loved playing baseball.

Taft was known for his many "firsts" in office. He was the first president to ride to his *inauguration* in an automobile. He was the first president to throw out a baseball at the opening of a Major League game. He was also the first president to play golf!

President Taft weighed more than 300 pounds. He was so big that a special bathtub had to be installed in the White House for him.

Taft left office after only one term. He was happy to go back to teaching law in college. But he was even happier when he was appointed Chief Justice of the Supreme Court. He was finally the judge he had always dreamed of becoming.

Governor James M. Cox of Dayton

Another poor boy who had struck it rich led the state in sweeping reforms. James Cox was a poor farm boy who had little education. But he worked hard and saved his money. He finally had enough money to buy a paper called the *Dayton Daily News*. He bought even more newspapers and became a very wealthy man.

Instead of retiring and enjoying his money, James Cox decided to run for governor of Ohio as a Democrat. Like many other people in his party, he liked the Progressive ideas. During the campaign, he promised to pass new laws that would help everyone. "We are entering upon a new day," was his stirring cry to the people of Ohio. He gave them courage to roll up their sleeves and work hard to make the future better.

Governor Cox passed two very important laws. One was called the ***minimum wage***. This law said workers must not be paid below a certain amount of money. It meant that more workers in Ohio would have enough money to take care of themselves and their families.

The other law was called ***workmen's compensation***. The law gave money to workers who were hurt on the job and had to stay home from work for a while.

Here are some of the many other reforms passed by Governor Cox:

James M. Cox

- Ended child labor.
- Improved country schools.
- Paved state roads.
- Gave more money to farmers.
- Hired school nurses and bus drivers.
- Made prices for electricity more fair.
- Made working in factories safer.

Flood Control

Governor Cox also worried about flooding in Ohio. Every spring Ohio's many rivers and streams overflowed their banks.

In March of 1913 the rain didn't stop for three terrible days. People called it the Great Flood of 1913. The worst flooding occurred in Governor Cox's hometown of Dayton. A wall of water twenty feet high rushed downtown. More than 400 people were drowned. Fires broke out when the flooding burst the town's gas lines.

Governor Cox started a dam-building project. Taxes were raised to pay for dams on rivers that often flooded. These dams were built first near Dayton, and then throughout the entire state.

Many other states watched how successful Ohio was in building dams. Soon they began similar projects.

Flooding waters near Cleveland caused a boat to knock down a bridge. When dams were built across the rivers, they let out the water a little at a time to prevent the flooding. The water behind the dams formed man-made lakes, or reservoirs.

Ohio Portrait

William Sidney Porter

William Porter was a bank clerk. The men who ran the bank where he worked stole all the money from the bank and left town. Porter was blamed for the crime. He did not want to go to prison so he ran away to another country. Then a letter came, telling him his wife was sick. He loved her very much and came back to America to be with her.

Porter was arrested and sentenced to three years in the Ohio State Prison in Columbus. He used his time to make himself a better person. He practiced writing short stories. When he left prison, he published his stories under a *pen name*. He called himself O. Henry.

Many of O. Henry's stories were about people who helped others. He called his best story "The Gift of the Magi." In the story, a young married couple love each other dearly. Christmas is coming. Each one wants to buy a nice present for the other one. But they are very poor. The young husband only has a pocket watch. The young woman has beautiful long hair but no money.

On Christmas Eve, they open their presents. The husband unwraps a beautiful chain for his watch. The wife receives a beautiful comb for her hair. They look at each other with love. The young man has sold his watch to buy the comb. The young wife has cut and sold her hair to buy the watch chain.

A pen name is a made-up name that an author uses instead of the author's real name. Can you think of a name you might use for your own pen name?

What do you think?

What do you think O. Henry was trying to show in this story? With your class, talk about love and sacrifice in a family.

157

The Wright Brothers

Wilbur Wright flies in 1908 over France.
Photo by North Wind Pictures

There was more going on in Ohio during this time than politics! The goal of progress and change for the better seemed to be everywhere. People wanted to invent new things that would make life better for everyone.

Wilbur and Orville Wright lived in Dayton. The brothers really loved machines. As young men, they made their own printing press out of a broken tombstone and old buggy parts. They went into business together printing a newspaper. Then they opened a bicycle shop. They made new bicycles and fixed old ones.

In their spare time, they experimented with flying machines. They watched birds in flight—especially buzzards. They saw that birds could go right or left. They could go up and down. They could also dip from one side to the other. The Wright Brothers knew a flying machine would have to do the same things.

The Wright Brothers' first airplane looked more like a kite than an airplane. They tested it over a cow pasture west of Dayton. A friend told them to take their plane to Kitty Hawk, North Carolina, where the wind currents were just right.

The brothers returned to Dayton to build a better flying machine. When they were ready, they took the plane to Kitty Hawk. They flipped a coin to see who would pilot the test flight. Orville won. That cold day in December, 1903, their two-winged glider with a small motor on board flew over the sand dunes. The first flight lasted 12 seconds! The plane flew only 120 feet, but those 120 feet made history.

Orville Wright (left)
Wilbur Wright (right)

Background photo by Middleton Evans

158

Three other flights lasted a little longer. The two brothers were very excited. They sent a telegram back home to their father in Dayton:

We have made four successful flights this morning . . . all against the wind. . . . We went up with engine power alone. . . . Our average speed through the air was 31 miles . . . our longest time in the air was 57 seconds!

The Wright Brothers returned home to Dayton. Many people still did not believe airplane flight was possible. Soon, however, planes were carrying passengers and mail between towns in Ohio.

Wilbur Wright gets ready to teach a student to fly.
Photo by North Wind Pictures

The Wright Sister

Did you know that Orville and Wilbur Wright had a sister who helped them with their inventions? Katharine Wright kept charts and graphs. She suggested ideas and helped with the experiments.

The Wright Brothers got angry when Katharine got engaged to be married. They thought that she would devote too much time to her new husband and not enough time to their flying machine project.

Dayton to Kitty Hawk

PENNSYLVANIA

OHIO
•Dayton
WEST VIRGINIA
KENTUCKY
VIRGINIA
Kitty Hawk
NORTH CAROLINA
SOUTH CAROLINA

Ohio Inventors

The Wright brothers were not the only inventors to come from Ohio. Look at the map and see how many inventors you can see.

An African American inventor named Granville Woods got the nickname the "Black Edison." Look at the list of some of his inventions, and see if you can tell why:

- Railway telegraph
- Amusement park rollercoaster
- Egg incubator (keeps chicken eggs warm so they will hatch)

Can you imagine starting a car by turning a crank on the car's front? That's how people did it when cars were first made. Then Charles Kettering invented the self-starter. After that, a car started when you turned the key.

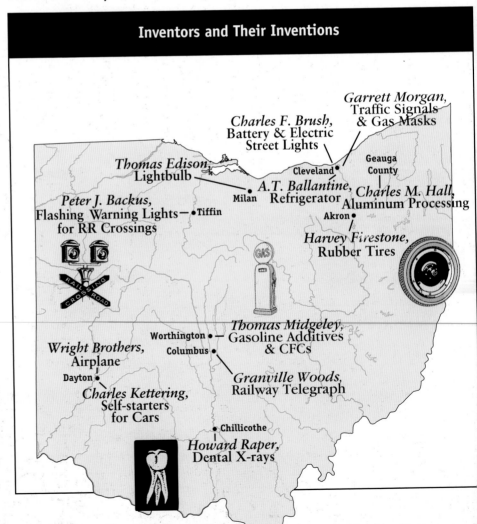

Inventors and Their Inventions

Garrett Morgan, Traffic Signals & Gas Masks

Charles F. Brush, Battery & Electric Street Lights

Thomas Edison, Lightbulb

Geauga County

Cleveland

A.T. Ballantine, Refrigerator
Milan

Charles M. Hall, Aluminum Processing

Peter J. Backus, Flashing Warning Lights for RR Crossings
Tiffin

Akron

Harvey Firestone, Rubber Tires

Wright Brothers, Airplane
Dayton

Worthington
Columbus

Thomas Midgeley, Gasoline Additives & CFCs

Charles Kettering, Self-starters for Cars

Granville Woods, Railway Telegraph

Chillicothe

Howard Raper, Dental X-rays

A Ku Klux Klan rally was held in Dayton in 1923. The men in white hoods burned crosses to scare people.

Trouble on the Horizon

Besides alcohol and prejudice, there were growing problems in business. Ohio and the nation were moving toward the *Great Depression* but no one knew it. Let's look at some of the things that were going wrong in Ohio:

• **Old Industries in Trouble:** People had been building trains for almost a century. There were now more railroads in Ohio than people could use. Many railroad companies were closing. Railroad workers were losing their jobs.

• **New Industries in Trouble:** Building cars and appliances were new industries in Ohio. So many cars were being made that there weren't enough people to buy them. Factories started to close. Workers were "laid off." This means they lost their jobs.

• **Farmers in Trouble:** Farmers in Ohio were growing more food than people could buy. Food prices were falling. Many farmers could no longer make a living by growing food. They had to sell their farms and move into the city.

The Stock Market Crash of 1929

People finally knew that businesses were in trouble on one terrible day. It happened in New York City at a place called Wall Street. People traded *stock* there. If you own stock, then you own part of a company. When business is good, stock prices go up. When business is bad, stock prices go down.

On October 29, 1929, everyone decided that business was bad. They all started selling their stock. Millions of shares were sold. Stock prices fell. By the end of that day, called Black Tuesday, most stocks were worthless.

The Great Depression had begun. The banks closed first. Many banks had invested all of their money in stocks. When the stocks became worthless, the banks lost all of their money. People who had their money in the banks were now broke. Soon many factories closed because no one had the money to buy anything. Many workers lost their jobs.

One out of every four workers in the United States had no job. The problem was much worse in Ohio. Look at the chart below. It shows how many people had no work in Ohio and its major cities.

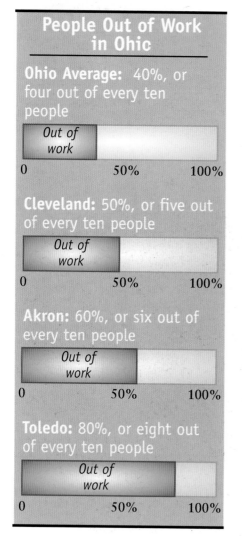

People Out of Work in Ohio

Ohio Average: 40%, or four out of every ten people

Out of work

0   50%   100%

Cleveland: 50%, or five out of every ten people

Out of work

0   50%   100%

Akron: 60%, or six out of every ten people

Out of work

0   50%   100%

Toledo: 80%, or eight out of every ten people

Out of work

0   50%   100%

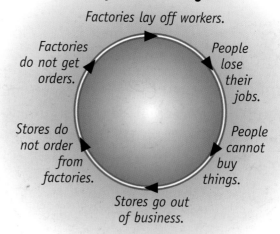

Depression Cycle

Factories lay off workers.

People lose their jobs.

People cannot buy things.

Stores go out of business.

Stores do not order from factories.

Factories do not get orders.

Ohio in the Great Depression

The Great Depression hit Ohio hard. Few people could buy cars, so many auto plants closed. Soon rubber factories closed too. Nearly every industry in Ohio made fewer goods. Many

WAR

...ND AND SEA. I HAVE SEEN
...HE WOUNDED... I HAVE
...MUD. I HAVE SEEN CITIES
...N CHILDREN STARVING.
...OF MOTHERS AND WIVES

End of a Century

WORDS TO UNDERSTAND
dictator
superior
inferior
concentration camp
draft
naval base
synthetic
toll road
tuition
income tax
lottery
segregate
civil rights
women's movement
journalist
communism
migrant workers
phosphates

What did President Roosevelt say about war? This is the FDR Monument in Washington, D.C.
Photo by Scott Barrow

1962
John Glenn becomes the first man to orbit the earth.

1972
United States and Canada clean up Lake Erie.

2000
A new millennium begins.

1998
John Glenn orbits the earth again.

1960s
Civil Rights Movement

1974
Ohio Lottery begins to raise money for schools.

| 1965 | 1970 | 1975 | 1980 | 1985 | 1990 | 1995 | 2000 |

1964–1975
Vietnam War

1971
Student protestors are killed at Kent State University.

1973
Ohio state income tax is adopted.

1975
VCRs (video cassette recorders) are first sold.

1990s
More and more computers are in homes and schools. The Internet is widely used.

World War II Begins

A *dictator* is the sole ruler of a country. Everyone must follow the orders of the dictator. There is little freedom in a country run by a dictator.

The United States was coming out of the Great Depression. President Roosevelt gave Americans the courage to face the future. His New Deal programs helped many people. Factories were opening again. People were going back to work. Everyone hoped the future would be better.

Most people knew that there was trouble in other parts of the world. A man named Adolf Hitler was the *dictator* of Germany. He was a member of the Nazi Party. The Nazis believed that the Germans were a *superior* race. They thought that other people were *inferior,* or not as good as the Germans. They thought people of some other races should be conquered or even killed.

Hitler especially disliked Jewish people. He sent millions of them to *concentration camps* in Europe. Six million Jews were put to death in the camps. Six million other people also died in Hitler's camps.

Concentration camps were prisons. Millions died at the camps.

Ohio men fought in Europe and Asia. Many were killed.

Hitler's army took over countries near Germany. Then his air force conquered Poland. England and France declared war on Hitler. Italy and Japan joined Germany. World War II had begun.

President Roosevelt prepared America for war. He started a peacetime *draft.* A draft is a law that requires people to serve in a war. He sent ships and supplies to help England. He warned Americans that someday they would have to fight Hitler.

182

The United States Enters the War

Sunday morning, December 7, 1941 was a beautiful one in Pearl Harbor, Hawaii. There were few clouds in the bright blue sky. Many large ships were tied up at the docks. Pearl Harbor was the most important *naval base* of the United States in the Pacific Ocean. The Navy had many ships there.

Suddenly the skies darkened. Wave after wave of Japanese fighter planes swooped down from the sky. They dropped bombs on the American ships. They gunned down the American sailors. Ships sank to the bottom of the ocean. Many young men were killed.

The next day, President Roosevelt asked Congress to declare war on Germany and Japan. The United States entered World War II

Choosing Leaders

Americans have an important right and responsibility to elect leaders who are honest and fair. Sometimes leaders have to make hard decisions, such as whether or not our country should go to war. Because these decisions are so important, our leaders must also have wisdom and courage.

- Talk with your teacher about what honesty, wisdom, and courage mean.
- Share your ideas on how President Roosevelt showed wisdom and courage at the start of the war.

After training in the United States, these soldiers went to Europe to stop Hitler's army.

Ohio Goes to War

Pilots trained at Wright-Patterson Air Force Base in Dayton.

Over 800,000 of Ohio's young men went off to fight. The men served in the U.S. Army, Air Force, Navy, and Marine Corps. Women supported the fighting men as secretaries, nurses, drivers and even pilots.

At home, the people of Ohio also worked hard to help the war effort. Some factories changed overnight. The Goodrich Tire and Rubber Company in Akron had made tires for cars. Once the war broke out, they switched to making airplanes. Thousands of fighter planes came off the assembly lines and headed for Germany and Japan.

Activity

Research Synthetic Rubber

Some scientists in Ohio helped invent *synthetic* rubber. This is rubber made by people instead of the natural rubber that comes from rubber trees. Without synthetic rubber, we could not have won the war. Do some research to learn more about rubber. What reference materials can you use? Try:

- An encyclopedia
- Library books
- The Internet

See if you can find out:
- Where does rubber come from?
- How do we get synthetic rubber?
- What is it used for?

Women and Children

With so many men off fighting the war, women went to work in the factories. They built ships and planes. Families also helped the troops. They planted "victory gardens" in their backyards. By growing vegetables at home, more food could be sent overseas to feed the troops.

College girls helped by joining an organization called the USO. They entertained troops at local army bases. They played cards, talked, and danced with the soldiers before the men were sent overseas.

184

Even children helped in the war effort. They collected tin cans and old tires. These were then recycled to make supplies like parachutes for the fighting men around the world.

World War II Ends

The terrible war finally ended in 1945. Sadly, President Roosevelt died just before it ended. When news of the victory reached the United States, the people of Ohio and all of America celebrated VE Day. VE stood for "Victory in Europe." All the church bells in Ohio rang out together. People paraded joyously through the streets.

Three months later, Japan surrendered. Americans celebrated VJ Day. VJ stood for "Victory in Japan." Once again the church bells rang and Ohioans celebrated.

Popeye Invents the Jeep

World War II was fought in many places. Soldiers needed a small truck that could travel on old paved roads, sandy deserts, and jungle pathways. Workers at the Willys-Overland Automobile Plant in Toledo developed a small truck to carry passengers and supplies. It could travel over all kind of roads.

The workers called it a Jeep after a character in "Popeye," a popular cartoon of the day. Popeye was a sailor. He had a magical dog named Jeep who could disappear and reappear anywhere. Could there be a better name for the sturdy little truck that could go anywhere?

The Atom Bomb

The United States used a new weapon called the atom bomb to defeat Japan. Captain Paul Tibbets of Columbus was the pilot of a plane called the *Enola Gay*. It flew over Japan with an atom bomb on board. The plane dropped the bomb on a city called Hiroshima. It completely destroyed the town in one terrible explosion.

A few days later, another American plane dropped an atom bomb on another Japanese city. It was a terrible blow for the Japanese people. But it ended the war with Japan. Luckily these terrible weapons have never again been used in wartime.

Captain Paul Tibbets flew the Enola Gay. *It dropped the atom bomb on Hiroshima.*

Ohio Faces the Future

World War II was over. The people of the state looked for ways to make Ohio better in the remaining decades of the twentieth century. Each decade took on a character all its own as the people of the state tackled one challenge after another.

New roads were built all over Ohio.

The 1950s: The Transportation Decade

The people of Ohio had worked hard to build roads, canals, and railroads. Later they paved their many roads for cars and trucks. Then they came up with even more ways to improve transportation.

• **Ohio Turnpike:** In Ohio's early history, the National Road had linked the state to the East and the West. Then the state needed an even bigger road to link Ohio to the rest of America. They built a multi-lane highway across the northern part of the state. They called it the Ohio Turnpike. A turnpike is a **toll road**. Drivers pay a fee to use it.

• **Federal Highway System:** The United States began a highway-building program. Ohio received millions of dollars to build highways. The new roads linked Ohio's major cities to each other. You can take I-75 in western Ohio all the way north to Canada and all the way south to Florida.

• **St. Lawrence Seaway:** The United States and Canada worked together to build a water route from the Great Lakes to the Atlantic Ocean. They called it the St. Lawrence Seaway. When it opened, it turned big cities on Lake Erie like Cleveland, Toledo, and Sandusky into international ports. They could ship cars, steel, coal, wheat, and corn to cities around the world.

New highways connected Ohio to the rest of the country.

The 1960s: The Education Decade

The people of Ohio knew they could only help America lead the world if her citizens had a good education. They tried to find ways to send everyone to college. They also came up with new ways to pay for public schools.

Thirteen state colleges were linked together to form the Ohio State University System. By the 1970s, every Ohio citizen was within thirty miles of a public college. Students paid low *tuition* to attend state colleges. The state gave tax dollars to the colleges to help pay for buildings, equipment, and teachers' salaries.

Ohio also came up with new ways to pay for public high schools and elementary schools. Governor John Gilligan, from Cincinnati, passed a state *income tax*. This meant that Ohio citizens gave part of their incomes to the state each year. Ohio used the money to pay for schools. The state even gave money to Ohio's many parochial schools.

The state also started a *lottery* to help pay for education. In a lottery, people buy tickets for one or two dollars a piece. A prize-winning ticket is drawn. People can win anywhere from a few dollars to millions of dollars in the Ohio lottery.

Ohio's State College System

University of Toledo
Cleveland State University
Bowling Green State University
Kent State University
University of Akron
Youngstown State University
Wright State University
Ohio State University
Central State University
Miami University
University of Cincinnati
Ohio University
Shawnee State University

Look at the map of Ohio's many state universities and colleges. Ohio has many other colleges and universities that are not on the map. Which of these universities is closest to your home?

Kindergarten school children in the 1960s wait until the bell rings so they can go home. Taxes and the lottery pay for schools.

187

Exploring Outer Space

Ohioans' love of transportation took them even farther in the 1960s. President John Kennedy challenged Americans to explore space. He even said the nation should land a man on the moon by 1970. Two Ohioans took up his challenge.

John Glenn Orbits the Earth

John Glenn was born in Cambridge, Ohio, but he grew up in a little town called New Concord. He attended Muskingum College. When World War II broke out, he joined the Marine Corps and became a pilot. He flew many combat missions in World War II and in the Korean War in Asia. He was a daring fighter pilot and received more than twenty medals for his bravery.

Later Glenn became a test pilot. He was the first man to fly faster than the speed of sound all the way from California to New York. Soon he was one of America's first astronauts.

Early on a February morning in 1962, John Glenn donned a space suit and climbed into a tiny capsule called the Friendship 7. A giant rocket shot the capsule into outer space off the coast of Florida. Americans waited anxiously in front of their televisions to hear news of John Glenn's flight. He orbited the earth three times before his capsule landed in the Atlantic Ocean. The whole flight had taken him only a little longer than his record-breaking trip across the United States by plane. John Glenn had become the first man to orbit the earth.

Glenn became a national hero and later a senator from Ohio. He returned to outer space when he was seventy-seven years old. He joined

Astronaut John Glenn gets into the space capsule.

At age seventy-seven, Senator
John Glenn again went into space.

the crew of the space shuttle Discovery and once again
orbited the earth. John Glenn proved that space travel
s for people of all ages.

NEIL ARMSTRONG WALKS ON THE MOON

Seven years after John Glenn first orbited the earth,
Americans were again glued to their television sets. Three
astronauts from the United States were in a spacecraft racing
toward the moon. Their mission was called Apollo XI. The
captain of the mission was a young man from Ohio. His name was
Neil Armstrong.

Armstrong came from Wapakoneta, Ohio. His family had
lived in western Ohio for a long time. As a boy, he loved science.
But when he grew up, he joined the navy and became a pilot. Like
John Glenn, he later became a test pilot and then an astronaut.

After the Apollo XI spacecraft began its orbit around the
moon, Armstrong guided a small landing craft called the Eagle
toward the surface of the moon. All the world heard Armstrong
radio back to earth, "Houston, Houston ... the Eagle has landed!"

When he finally came down the ladder and walked on the
moon, Armstrong said these famous words: "That's one small
step for man—one giant leap for mankind!"

Neil Armstrong later came back to western Ohio and to his
love of science. He taught math and science at the University of

Astronaut Neil Armstrong was the first
man to walk on the moon.

The Moon and Your Computer

We can thank the first moon landing for the personal computer that we now call a PC. Before 1969, computers were very large. They were as big as a room or even as large as a building. American scientists knew that a much smaller computer would be needed for landing men on the moon.

The *Eagle* was the landing craft that took Neil Armstrong and Buzz Aldrin to the moon's surface. Large computers on the earth could direct the *Apollo XI* spacecraft, but a tiny computer would have to be built to take inside the *Eagle*. Computer engineers built the small computer. It helped Neil Armstrong guide the *Eagle* to the moon's surface. It helped him get it safely back to the spacecraft.

That computer became the model for all personal computers used in homes, schools, and businesses today. Not only had the *Eagle* landed, so had the PC!

Young African American leaders worked hard to end segregation. One leader was Dr. Martin Luther King Jr., a Baptist minister from Georgia. He organized peaceful protests and led marches against segregation.

Civil Rights

For many years, blacks and whites in much of America were separated, or *segregated* from each other. There were separate schools for black children and white children. Black people had to sit in the back of buses and trains. "White Only" or "Colored Only" was printed on signs above water fountains.

In Ohio, black families were not welcome in many neighborhoods. Blacks could not sit down to eat in many restaurants. They could go to movie theaters, but they had to sit upstairs in the balconies.

Even most hotels were segregated. When Marian Anderson, a famous black opera singer, came to Toledo in the 1930s, the best hotel in town turned her away. She had to go across the street to another hotel.

President John Kennedy proposed major *civil rights* laws to end discrimination. Civil rights are rights of personal liberty.

Getting an Education and Good Jobs

While poverty remains a problem, many young black people

190

Factors of Production

There are four things that must come together before something is sold as a good or service. These things are called *factors of production*. Factors of production are:

- Land
- Labor
- Entrepreneurship
- Capital goods

Find the rubber plant and the place the bicycle seats come from. Find the workers putting on the tires. How are the bikes taken to the store? Find the consumer taking a new bike home. Pretend you see a boy in another country far away riding one of the new bikes.

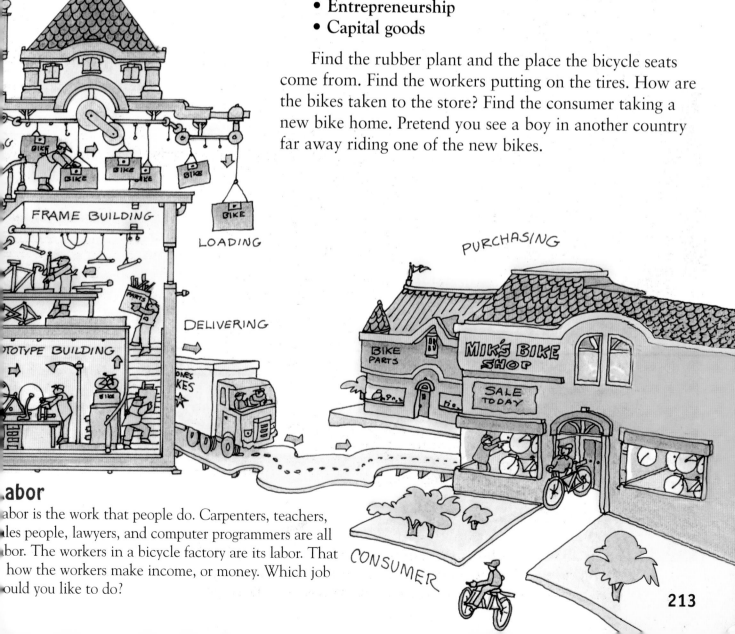

Labor

Labor is the work that people do. Carpenters, teachers, sales people, lawyers, and computer programmers are all labor. The workers in a bicycle factory are its labor. That is how the workers make income, or money. Which job would you like to do?

Transportation and Trade

Transportation of natural resources and finished products is very important for business. Without good transportation, business would almost stop.

Columbus Airport was opened in 1929. Would you like to ride in one of these airplanes?

- **Airports:** Every big town in Ohio has a modern airport. The Wright Brothers gave the state a head start in flight. They were the first entrepreneurs to build airplanes for commercial use. Columbus was the first American city to begin flights for passengers.

- **Railroads:** Trains still crisscross the state just like they did more than a hundred years ago. They bring goods into Ohio and take manufactured items and farm products out of the state. The Lake Shore Limited is one of the most important passenger routes in the country. It runs along the Lake Erie shoreline. The train carries people all the way east to New York and Boston, and all the way west to San Francisco.

- **Roads and Highways:** Roads have been important to Ohio since the early days of settlement. The National Road cut through the center of the state. It linked Ohio to the older states back east and the newer ones out west. Road building never stopped in Ohio. Today major interstates and the Ohio Turnpike still link Ohio to the rest of the nation just like the old National Road once did.

Do you live in or near a large city? Have you ever been in a traffic jam? We all like to get to where we are going quickly. Freeways help people get in and out of Cleveland and other Ohio cities.

Enjoying Ohio!

When people visit Ohio from other states and countries, they may eat at the Old Navy Bistro in Toledo, visit the Rock and Roll Hall of Fame and Museum in Cleveland, go to the Cedar Point Amusement Park in Sandusky, or cheer at a Cincinnati Reds baseball game. This is all part of tourism—a major industry in Ohio.

Tourism provides jobs and money because people come to Ohio and spend money on transportation, lodging, food, entertainment, and recreation. All of the things tourists do in our state make money for the businesses and workers of Ohio.

Tourists love to visit this replica of Columbus's ship, the Santa Maria. Can you guess which Ohio city has the ship?

Photo by John D. Ivanko

Racing over the track along Lake Erie at sixty-five miles per hour, Cedar Point's Mean Streak was the tallest and fastest wooden roller coaster in the world when it came to Sandusky in 1991. If you were a tourist, would you ride the Mean Streak?

Photo by Dan Feicht

The Ohio Adventure

This book is a good example of how economics and world trade work. Ohio's students needed a new Ohio history book. An entrepreneur started a book publishing company. The owner of the company and his employees decided that they wanted to make a book that children would really like. They worked hard to make it interesting and tell a true story of Ohio. They also hoped the teachers would like the book enough to buy it, so the company would make a profit.

It took the services and products of many people in different parts of the world to make the book. Here is what happened.

The author in Ohio studied Ohio's history. She went to libraries and read books about Ohio. She read the diaries of people who had lived here a long time ago. The author wrote the words on a computer. The editor in Utah was in charge of making sure the spelling and punctuation were right. Another person found the photographs. She lives in New York. An artist drew some of the pictures. A different artist used a computer to arrange the words and pictures on each page. All of these things took over a year to do.

When the book was ready to be printed, it was sent across the Pacific Ocean to Korea. The paper came from trees in Asia. Someone made and sold the ink to the printer. Many workers there printed the book on huge presses. They used machines to sew the pages together and glue the covers on. After about four months the books were brought to America on a ship. The ship landed in San Francisco. Then large boxes of books were brought to Ohio in trucks.

Making a book is an adventure! It is part of the economics of Ohio and other places in the world.

All of the people who worked on the book had to be paid for their services. All of the machines, computers, paper, and even ink had to be paid for. Where did the money come from?

You and your friends are the consumers. Your school paid for your books. The schools got the money from the government. The government got the money from taxes. The taxes were paid by the adults in your town. The people earned the money to pay their taxes from their jobs or businesses.

So there you have it. People work hard to provide the goods and services other people need. The work makes them feel good about themselves. It provides money for the workers and their families. The work helps provide for the needs of everyone.

Goods and Services

Goods are things that are usually manufactured. This means they are made in factories, workshops, or even at home. They are then sold for money. Shoes, pencils, televisions, and dog collars are all goods. People make money by making and selling goods.

Services are things that people do for other people. Dentists, sales clerks, umpires, coaches, and your teacher are providing services. People earn money by providing services.

Don't be fooled! Many people who provide a service also use goods. The sales clerk, for example, is providing a service by selling shoes. The shoes are goods, but the sales clerk provides a service by selling them to you.

On a separate piece of paper, number from one to fourteen. Write **G** for goods or **S** for services for each job listed below.

1. Works with plumbing
2. Collects the garbage
3. Teaches students
4. Manufactures paint
5. Paints pictures to sell
6. Makes engines for cars
7. Repairs cars
8. Wraps cheese in a factory
9. Delivers cheese to grocery stores
10. Makes telephones
11. Repairs telephones
12. Manufactures light bulbs
13. Sells light bulbs
14. What you would like to do when you grow up

Chapter 12 Review

1. If you work for someone else, you are an _____.
2. How do Ohio businesses make a profit?
3. What is supply and demand?
4. A person who buys things is called a _____.
5. What are the four factors of production?
6. Name one Ohio entrepreneur and the product that the entrepreneur made.
7. List two types of transportation and why each is so important to Ohio's businesses.
8. What are the two main crops grown in Ohio today?
9. List at least three jobs that provide services. Tell why they are services, not goods.
10. How do tourists help make money for Ohio?

Geography Tie-In

Take a look at the list of Ohio's major companies. What company is nearest your town and school? If you wanted to start a new company in Ohio, what city would you locate it in and why?

Chapter 13

THE TIME
1776–2000

PEOPLE TO KNOW
George Washington
James Madison
Alexander Hamilton
George Voinovich
Mike DeWine
Marcy Kaptur
Bob Taft

PLACES TO LOCATE
Philadelphia
Washington, D.C.
Columbus

Timeline of Events

1776
The United States declares independence from Great Britain.

1787
The U.S. Constitution is written.

1788
The U.S. Constitution is ratified.

1803
Ohio enters the Union as the seventeenth state.

1750 — 1775 — 1800 — 1825

1775-1783
Revolutionary War

1802
Men at Ohio's first Constitutional Convention wrote our state constitution.

City Government

Another kind of local government even closer to home is city government. Cities are usually run by a mayor or a city manager, with a city council.

Cities make rules about what kinds of buildings can be built in different regions of the city. They often keep houses separate from businesses. They make sure schools are in safe places. They make laws about speed limits on the roads.

African American Leaders

African Americans continue to do great things in Ohio government. Jack Ford was elected mayor of Toledo in 2001. Before he was mayor, he worked for seven years in the state legislature. Other people of color hold important offices in state, county, and city government.

Vote for Me!

At election time, it is the responsibility of the citizens to vote for leaders who will be fair, reliable (do what they promise), tell the truth, and make wise decisions. Voters need to choose leaders who have the courage to stand up for what they believe is right even if others disagree. Would you vote for this kind of a leader?

I'll Do It!

People do not have to win an election to help their community. Many people are glad they live in Ohio and want to make it a better place. Volunteers work without being paid. They work in hospitals and teach English to immigrants. They take care of children and deliver food to people with disabilities. They give tours at museums. They help teachers in schools and give music programs at homes for the elderly. Volunteers pick up trash along the road and plant flowers and trees. Have you ever been a volunteer?

As a class, make a list of things that you could volunteer to do. Then work to make your community better.

County and city governments are local governments. They are close to home.

Most cities have an ordinance, or law, that says dogs must have a license and cannot run loose around the neighborhood.

Part of our democratic form of government is voting for good leaders and telling our leaders what we want them to do.

239

Taxes Pay for Services

Ohio's constitution gives our state, counties, and cities the power to collect taxes. Tax money helps pay for services all the people can use. Taxes come in many forms. People and businesses pay taxes on the money they make. When you buy clothes or toys, you pay a sales tax. Each county collects taxes on land, homes, and buildings. These are called property taxes.

What is tax money used for? Taxes pay for making and fixing local streets. They pay for plowing snow. Taxes pay for libraries where you can check out books. Cities use tax money to pay for clean water. They have garbage picked up. If you play soccer on a city team or swim in a city pool, you are using a city service. Cities also pay for parks where you can play ball and have picnics.

Taxes pay for public education. If you go to a public school, your building, your books, and your teachers are paid with tax money. If you go to a private school, your parents pay for most of these things.

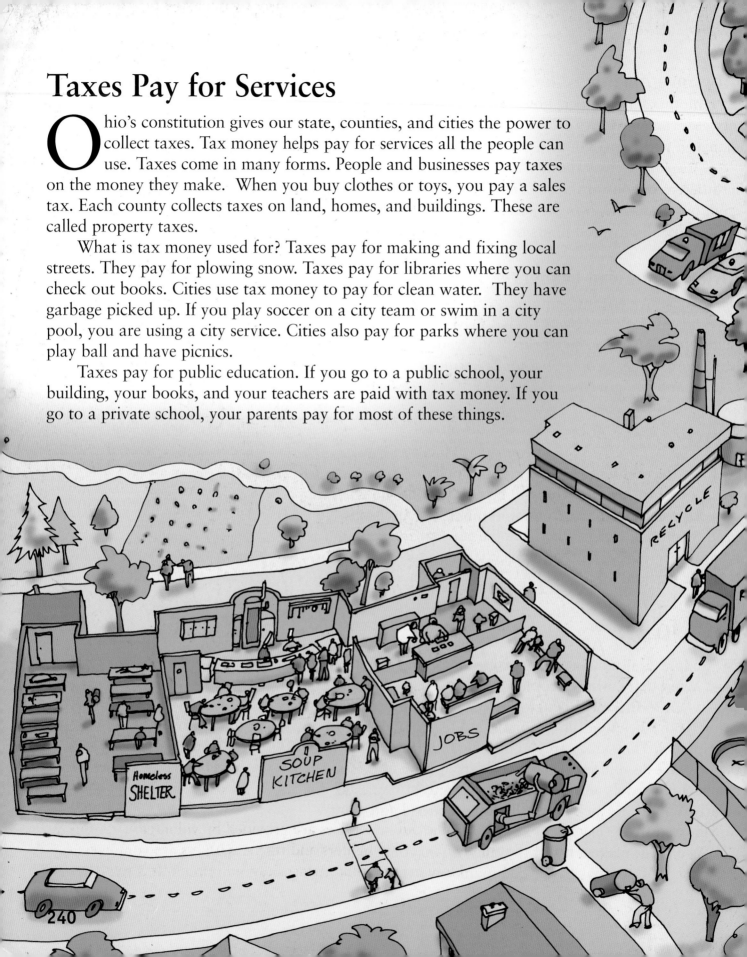

Some public services are provided by volunteers. In Ohio, many of our fire fighters and rescue workers are volunteers. How many public services can you find in this town?

Activity

Get Involved!

Ohio is only as good as its people. That means all of the people—men and women, rich and poor, young and old—must be good citizens. They need to obey the law. They must respect the rights of others. They should be reliable and keep their promises. They need to get involved in government and help others whenever they can.

Here are some things you can do. Discuss these ideas as a class. What other things can you do? Make a list on the board.

- Obey all of your family and school rules.
- Tell the truth and be honest.
- Be polite and fair to everyone.
- Help keep your own home and yard clean.
- Volunteer to help others.
- Join civic, community, and service organizations.
- Never ruin property.
- Ask adults in your family to vote.
- Tell your representatives what you want them to do (by letter or e-mail).
- Write a letter to the editor of a newspaper. Letters from kids often get published!
- Talk with adults about what is going on in government, especially in your town.

Chapter 13 Review

1. When did the Founding Fathers declare independence from Great Britain?
2. What important document did George Washington and other leaders write?
3. What are the three branches of government in the United States?
4. In the United States we elect _____ to vote for us in government meetings.
5. Who are the current senators from Ohio?
6. Name the two main political parties.
7. What important document was written by the Ohio State Constitutional Conventions?
8. A _____ is when the governor refuses to sign a bill.
9. A _____ or a _____ decides if a person is guilty of a crime.
10. What are some city and county services?
11. List at least three things that tax money is used for.

Geography Tie-In

On a wall map in your classroom, locate Washington, D.C. (our national capital), and Columbus (our state capital).

- How far do our representatives have to travel to get to Washington?
- What are some of the ways our representatives might travel? What states might they drive through or fly over?

GLOSSARY

The definitions given here are for the **Terms To Understand** as they are used in this textbook. The words appear in bold italic print the first time they occur in the book.

abolitionist: a person who worked to eliminate slavery

abundant: a great number of something

advertising: selling goods and services through TV, radio, and printed ads

agriculture: farming; raising crops and livestock to sell for food

ambassador: an official sent to represent one country in another country

annuities: yearly payments

archaeologist: a scientist who learns about ancient people by studying the things they left behind

archaic: very old

artifact: an object made by people long ago

assassinated: to be murdered by sudden or secret attack

atlatl: a spear thrower

average: the number you get when you add up numbers and then divide the sum by the total amount of numbers; a typical amount

bestseller: a book that sells very well

bill: a written idea for a law

canal: a waterway made by people rather than nature

candidate: a person who seeks an office

charter: a document written when a colony is started

civil rights: the rights that belong to every citizen

climate: the weather of a place over a long period of time

colony: a territory under the control of another nation

communal: used or shared by everyone in a group

concentration camp: a camp where prisoners were kept, tortured, and killed

concentric: having a common center; circles within circles

confederation: a group united for a common purpose

consumer: a person who buys and uses things

consumer good: goods, such as clothing and cars, that people buy and use

continent: one of the seven large land areas of the world

correspondence course: a course taken through the mail

country: a land region under the control of one government

county: a region that has certain government powers; part of a state

cremate: to burn to ashes

dictator: a ruler with absolute power

dishonest: not honest; untrustworthy

divide: a ridge of high ground between drainage areas

draft: to force into military service

economics: how goods and services are made, distributed, and used

effigy: a work of art in the shape of a living thing

elementary: simple; basic

emigrate: to leave your home country and move to another one

employee: a person who works for wages

entrepreneur: a person who organizes, manages, and assumes the risk of a business

erode: to wear away the land by wind or water

expense: a cost; money spent

extinct: animals or plants that no longer exist anywhere on the earth

factors of production: land, labor, capital, and entrepreneurship; the things that must come together before goods are made and sold

federal: a strong national government where powers are also held by states

flatboat: a large wooden raft with a small cabin

fort: an area enclosed by a wooden stockade for protection

free enterprise: a system where the people, not just the government, run businesses for profit

free state: a state that did not allow slavery

geography: the study of the land, water, plants, animals, people, and locations of a place

geologist: a scientist who studies the history of the earth through rock formations

geometric: resembling shapes such as rectangles and squares

German: people from Germany

glacier: a large thick mass of ice built up over a long period of time

goods: products that are made, bought, and sold

grade school: a school with grades one through eight

Great Depression: a time in the 1930s when the economy was poor and many people could not make enough money to support themselves

Great Spirit: the god or spirit the American Indians believed watched over them

habitat: the natural place where a plant or animal lives

headwaters: the place where a river begins

high school: a school with grades nine through twelve

historic: people about whom we have a history, (written by people who lived at that time)

human features: things such as buildings and roads that people build on the land

humid: a weather condition where the air is very moist and uncomfortable to people

imitate: to copy

immigrant: a person who moves into a new country

import: to bring goods into one country from another country

inaugurate: to swear into office

inauguration: a ceremony to swear an official into office

income tax: a tax placed on a person's salary or wage

independence: freedom from the control or rule of another country or person

Independent: a member of no political party; not a Republican or a Democrat

industry: having to do with work, factories, and businesses

inferior: lower in social position

Irish: people from Ireland

journalist: a person who writes for a newspaper or magazine

jury: citizens who decide a case in a courtroom

kame: a small mound of gravel left by retreating glaciers

keelboat: a round-bottomed boat with the front curved into a point

labor union: a group of workers who join together to cause change

landslide: an election in which one candidate wins by a large majority

lavish: very fancy

legend: a story passed down through the ages

legislator: a person elected to make laws

local: near home

lock: an enclosure used to raise or lower boats as they pass through different water levels

longhouse: a large oblong house made with poles and animal skins

lottery: a way to raise money in which tickets are sold and a drawing is held to find the winner of a very large amount of money

majority: a number greater than half

migrant workers: people who move from place to place in order to find work

minimum wage: the lowest hourly wage that the law allows to be paid to an employee

Mound Builders: American Indians who built large earthen mounds

natural environment: the natural outdoor habitat of a plant or animal

naval base: a place where people in the navy live and work

neutral: not taking either side

nominate: to choose someone to run as a candidate in an election

orator: a public speaker

ordinance: a city rule or law

paleo: ancient

paralyze: to lose movement in a body part

parochial school: a school run by a church

pen name: a name an author uses when he doesn't want to use his own name

permanent: something that lasts a very long time

phosphates: acids that pollute water; materials used in soap and fertilizer

pioneer: a person who is among the first to enter and settle a region

plantation: a large farming estate

political party: a group of people who have a lot of the same ideas about government

politics: the activities and ideas of government

precipitation: water that falls to earth as rain or snow

prehistoric: people about whom we have no history that was written at the time

prejudice: an opinion made before the facts are known; a judgment made about someone just on the basis of race or religion

preserve: a place set apart to protect animals and plants

processed food: foods that have been prepared and preserved in a factory; canned, frozen, or packaged fruit, vegetables, soup, cereal, cookies, and so on

profit: the money made after expenses are paid

Progressive: a political party; people who work for social changes

prohibition: forbidding the manufacture, sale, and drinking of alcoholic beverages

public school: a school open to all children and paid for with money from taxes

railroad: a road with tracks for trains to travel on

reform: to change in order to make a situation better

region: a place or land division that has certain common characteristics (landforms, weather, etc.)

representative: a person who has been elected to vote for other people

representative democracy: a form of government where a person (representative) is elected to vote on behalf of other people

republic: a system of government in which citizens elect their own leaders

reservation: an area of land where the U.S. government forced American Indians to live

retreat: to withdraw or back off

running mate: a candidate who runs for office with another candidate, such as a vice-president

sailboat: a boat with sails powered by wind

salary: money paid to an employee

sales tax: a tax on a purchase

scandal: a public disgrace that may damage a reputation

sea-to-sea clause: a document that says that a colony owns all the land from its eastern border to the Pacific Ocean

sediment: the material (such as sand and rocks) left behind by water, wind, or a glacier

segregate: to separate by race

semi-permanent: long-lasting but not forever

services: acts done for another person

shaman: a medicine man and religious leader

slave: a person who is owned by another person and is forced to work without pay

slave state: a state in which slavery was legal and common

speakeasy: a place selling alcohol illegally during prohibition

state capital: the city where the main state government activities take place

steamboat: a boat with a large paddle wheel, powered by steam

stock: money invested in a business

stockbroker: someone who buys and sells stocks for other people

streetcar: a vehicle that runs on rails along city streets

strip mine: to clear off trees and earth to remove minerals

suburb: a community next to a city

superior: higher in social position

supply and demand: an economic term that relates the selling price of goods to how much is available for sale and how much people are willing to pay to get it

sympathy: sharing the feelings of others

synthetic: made by chemicals rather than nature

tariff: a tax placed on imported goods

temperate: not excessive or extreme

temporary: lasting for a short time

tenement: a rundown, low-rental apartment building

tepee: an American Indian home made of tall poles and animal skins

till: soil left from a glacier; a mixture of clay, sand, and gravel

toll road: a road a person has to pay to use

township: a division of land

treaty: a formal agreement between two groups or countries

troops: soldiers sent to fight in war

tuition: money paid to attend school

veterinary: having to do with the health of animals

veto: to reject a government bill; to say "no"

vision quest: a journey an Indian boy went on to learn about himself

wage: money paid to employees

wigwam: a hut made of poles overlaid with bark, grass mats, or hides

women's movement: a time in which women fought for equal rights

workmen's compensation: money paid to an employee who was hurt on the job (It is called "worker's compensation" today.)

INDEX